PRAISE FOR

YOUR MIND IS WHAT YOUR BRAIN DOES FOR A LIVING

"In our most private moments, we all see the patterns in our lives that hold us back. But what we don't see clearly is how they were set in motion or how to go about changing things. Fogel lays out a blueprint for both—a map with easy-to-follow exercises designed to reset 'faulty wiring' and create the potential to live healthier, more accepting, and more loving lives."

—CONNELL COWAN, PH.D., COAUTHOR
OF *SMART WOMEN/FOOLISH CHOICES*

"How can you choose from the flurry of self-help books that attempt to help us navigate through our rapidly changing times? The beauty of this book resides in its comprehensive appreciation of how we can control the timeless unconscious patterns of our childhoods right up to how the current contributions of the neurosciences can help us live more peacefully in the present."

—FRED M. SANDER, M.D., ASSOCIATE CLINICAL PROFESSOR,
DEPARTMENT OF PSYCHIATRY, WEILL CORNELL MEDICAL COLLEGE,
AND AUTHOR OF *INDIVIDUAL AND FAMILY THERAPY*

"Fogel provides a compelling 'playbook' on a way to achieve a full and rewarding life."

—FRANK MANCUSO, FORMER CHAIRMAN AND CEO,
PARAMOUNT PICTURES AND MGM STUDIOS

"Among the many wise messages in Steve Fogel's book is that in order to nurture those you love, you must first nurture yourself. To learn how best to do that, turn to page 1 and keep reading."

—ANN PLESHETTE MURPHY, PARENTING EDUCATOR
AND AUTHOR OF *THE 7 STAGES OF MOTHERHOOD*

"Steve Fogel's book serves as a practical bridge between understanding oneself and making the necessary changes for a more meaningful life. As a psychiatrist, I can say that it does so by providing building blocks for constructive self-awareness in a most accessible and organized fashion."

—DIANE WEISS, M.D.

"Steve Fogel shows the reader how to live a successful and balanced life full of purpose. I am impressed that his positive and educated messaging will help many find their own roads to success."

—TOM GORES, FOUNDER, CHAIRMAN, AND CEO, PLATINUM EQUITY, LLC

"Every day our volunteer coaching program assists young adults seeking jobs in a difficult economy. By the time they find us, these college grads have met with so much rejection or lack of responsiveness from the workplace that they feel anxious and utterly defeated. I can think of no better way to help them regain hope and agency than to recommend this book. Rather than feel like victims, they learn to understand their own thought processes, let go of self-defeating patterns, make mindful choices, and increase inner strength. What an enormous gift to a young person starting out in life!"

—WENDY SCHUMAN, FOUNDER, GRAD LIFE CHOICES, AND FORMER EXECUTIVE EDITOR, *PARENTS* MAGAZINE

"Bringing together the latest neuroscience, mind/body work, cognitive/ behavioral psychology, and the science and art of mindfulness, Steven Fogel's most recent book presents any reader the direction and tools to climb out of the trap that keeps one from achieving a more fulfilling, transformative, and creative life."

—ROLAND A. FRAUCHIGER, M.A., M.F.T.

YOUR MIND IS

WHAT YOUR

BRAIN DOES

FOR A LIVING

YOUR MIND IS

WHAT YOUR

BRAIN DOES

FOR A LIVING

....

Learn How to Make It Work for You

STEVEN JAY FOGEL

with MARK BRUCE ROSIN

GREENLEAF
BOOK GROUP PRESS

Published by Greenleaf Book Group Press
Austin, Texas
www.gbgpress.com

Distributed by Greenleaf Book Group LLC

For ordering information or special discounts for bulk purchases, please contact Greenleaf Book Group LLC at
PO Box 91869, Austin, TX 78709, 512.891.6100.

Design and composition by Greenleaf Book Group LLC
Cover design by Kuo Design
Brain illustration by ©iStockphoto.com/nicoolay

Publisher's Cataloging-In-Publication Data
Fogel, Steven Jay, 1942-
   Your mind is what your brain does for a living : learn how to make it work for you / Steven Jay Fogel with Mark Bruce Rosin. — 1st ed.
      p. ; cm.
   A follow-up to My mind is not always my friend.
   Issued also as an ebook.
   ISBN: 978-1-62634-058-9
   1. Choice (Psychology) 2. Control (Psychology) 3. Self-consciousness (Awareness) 4. Interpersonal relations. I. Fogel, Steven Jay, 1942- My mind is not always my friend. II. Rosin, Mark Bruce. III. Title.
BF611 .F64 2014
153.8   2013952322

Part of the Tree Neutral® program, which offsets the number of trees consumed in the production and printing of this book by taking proactive steps, such as planting trees in direct proportion to the number of trees used: www.treeneutral.com

Printed in the United States of America on acid-free paper   TreeNeutral®

14 15 16 17 18 19   10 9 8 7 6 5 4 3 2 1

First Edition

All of my life lessons have come out of my experience with my family. I would like to dedicate this book to my mother, Leah, and my children, Melinda, Nicole, Kelly, and Blake.

"The unexamined life is not worth living."

—Socrates, as quoted in *The Apology* by Plato

CONTENTS

ACKNOWLEDGMENTS

I would like to thank Ron Levine, Ph.D., Robin L. Kay, Ph.D., Cynthia Hoppenfeld, Brookes Nohlgren, Sharon Goldinger, and Michael Levin for their contributions to this book and to my life. And, of course, I would like to thank my coauthor, Mark Bruce Rosin, for his enduring friendship and extraordinary collaboration.

INTRODUCTION

As a result of the rapid evolution of technological intelligence, we find ourselves living in a time of unprecedented innovation. These technological advances bring incredible benefits, yet, at the same time, the exponential rate of change they've produced is so great I believe it's upsetting our mental equilibrium as individuals and the equilibrium of the world as a whole.

Imagine what it was like living in 1491 when people thought the Earth was flat and that if you went to the edge of it you would fall off. Then, in 1492, Columbus sailed to the Americas. It took thirty-three days for him to make the voyage and almost seven weeks in 1493 to sail back to Europe with the news that the Earth was round. That was a sea change for humankind's understanding of the planet, and it took a long time to occur. Now it seems as though sea changes are happening every five minutes.

Technology has changed everything in our lives and will continue to do so at speeds previously unheard of. Digital and cellular/Internet connectivity have revolutionized communication and made it easy to be in touch instantaneously with anything or anyone anywhere. We don't need to remember as many personal facts—birthdays, phone numbers, appointments—as we used to or even do simple calculations since our smartphones perform these functions for us. We don't have to remember other types of general facts, either, because they are instantly available on the Internet.

People who aren't computer, Internet, and smartphone literate are increasingly isolated from those who are. Technology has changed the economy by simultaneously creating and eliminating jobs in every field. Frequently we now deal with digital voices, making much of our lives literally impersonal, as well as frustrating and alienating.

Digital communication and social networking were the backbone of the Arab Spring uprisings of 2012 that led to changes in government and gave us a view of history as it was actually happening. But in America many of us are confused about what is really happening and what it all means because the reporting and commentaries of Internet columnists, bloggers, and political organizations are so partisan and conflicting that it's hard to tell fact from fiction.

We worry about identity theft, viruses, phishing for our money. We worry about credit reports, and with good reason: *One out of five* credit reports contains a mistake, and the credit-rating agencies and credit card companies have a dismal record of correcting them.[1]

As our lives have become increasingly computerized, we have also become increasingly enmeshed with numbers. We're identified by our Social Security number, the number on our driver's license, and the numbers on our credit cards and bank accounts. We have passwords to open our computer, to open our email, and for our various bank and online purchasing accounts.

All of this—not just the things we worry about individually but the change itself—creates anxiety at both a personal and a global level. So many far-reaching technological innovations have arrived in such a short time, and so many keep arriving, that we haven't connected the dots to tell us how to cope with such massive change. Our society has not yet created the mental infrastructure needed to integrate all the changes, and this creates an underlying nervousness that affects all of us.

Long before the onset of our Digital Age, I became interested in discovering methods for creating a happier life in order to "fix" what seemed to be broken in my own inner world. Growing up, I'd always assumed that having money would bring happiness and peace of mind. At thirty, I found that I'd achieved my dream of money and success, but I was still anxious and frustrated, and despite being married, having two wonderful children, and being surrounded by friends and business colleagues and the luxuries my wealth afforded me, I felt isolated and alone.

Through therapy, self-actualization workshops, and self-examination and reflection, I learned that the only way I could fix what seemed to be broken in my inner world was to learn how my inner world had been formed, how it limited me, and about the power I had to change it.

I learned that we human beings unconsciously develop patterns of thinking and acting in childhood that, by the time we're adults, become our programmed strategies to "handle" the world. Unless we become aware of our individual programming and learn to interrupt it, this programming runs us on automatic pilot and, without our realizing it, determines our beliefs and behavior.

This is radically different from how we generally think about our beliefs and behavior.

Most of us think that our conscious mind—which we believe is responding accurately to whatever is happening here and now—is the source of our beliefs, and that our beliefs are true because the voice in our head tells us they are. We also believe we act the way we do because it's right or because that's just the way we have to act— again, the voice in our head tells us that's the way it is.

The reality is that the coping strategies we learned as children, many of which we may not even be aware of, are so ingrained and powerful that *until we learn to focus our attention in the present to make mindful decisions, these habitual coping strategies are the source of what we think and how we act and react.* I call these ingrained childhood coping strategies our *default programming*, or, as I referred to it earlier, simply our *programming.*

The problem with our default programming is that it's often dysfunctional. That's why earlier when I talked about strategies to handle the world, I put the word *handle* in quotes, because the way our default programming handles the world is often self-defeating.

Here's why: When our default programming is running us, even though we think we're in the here and now, we're not in the here and now at all; we're just repeating past behaviors that keep us in the past and rob us of what we want in the present.

That's why, at age thirty, after achieving everything I'd always dreamed about, I was still unhappy; internally I was still the same unhappy child, unaware that I was being run by the same default programming that had made me an unhappy child.

Fortunately, through the work I've undertaken since then, I've learned how we can identify our self-defeating programming and how we can learn to think and act in ways that work for us instead of against us. The process of recognizing your dysfunctional patterns of thinking and behaving and replacing them with healthier ones that make you happier and more fulfilled is *self-transformation*.

Self-transformation and steps for accomplishing it are the subject of the first book in this series, *My Mind Is Not Always My Friend: A Guide for How to Not Get in Your Own Way*. I wrote it to share the lessons I'd learned to that point, which had helped me increase the happiness in my life. The positive feedback I've gotten from readers and from the many people I mentor professionally and personally inspired me to write this second book to share additional lessons I've discovered about how your default programming can sabotage you without your you knowing it and about how to interrupt it and make choices to act in healthier ways that will help you achieve your goals and create more joy in your life.

Let me stop for a minute here to say that you don't need to have read book one in order to benefit from *Your Mind Is What Your Brain Does for a Living*. Each book stands alone and is a companion book for the other. In this new book, I further explore and refine the fundamental concepts outlined in *My Mind Is Not Always My Friend*. In addition, I share what I've learned about the valuable findings of neuroscientists about the human brain and how our minds work. You'll see why the structure and the functioning of the brain allow us to transform ourselves in ways that help us to become happier and more fulfilled.

In Part I, I explain how your default programming is formed and how it influences the way you think and act. In Part II, I share with you what the current research in neuroscience—the life science that studies the brain and the nervous system (*neuro* means "nerve")—has revealed to us about how our thought processes and behaviors are related to how our brain works. In Part III, I discuss what I've learned about how to resolve long-term dysfunctional relationships and situations—which I call frog-in-hot-water experiences—that cause stress, frustration, and pain. In Part IV, I share with you tools and techniques for disengaging from your dysfunctional programming and leading a fulfilling life. I conclude the book with five shorthand messages for you as you embark on the journey to live a fuller life of authenticity and aliveness.

..... 🧠 .....

Several years ago I went to a lecture given by Deborah Szekely, founder of the Golden Door, a retreat in California that focuses on balancing mind, body, and spirit. Deborah, who was then eighty-four years old, spoke to us about being ageless. Her main message was to look at each day's elective experiences and see whether each particular experience is enhancing your life or diminishing it: If it's diminishing it, don't do it; do only those things that enhance your life.

In *The Art of Living*, the Dalai Lama points out that certain things that may give you pleasure, such as the rush from gambling, drugs, or promiscuous sex, aren't good for you, and he contrasts these with the pleasure gained from love or from a job well done. He explains that one way to know if an action is worth doing is to ask yourself, before you do it, if ultimately the act will give you inner peace. He advises you to do only those things that will give you inner peace since they are the only things that are truly pleasurable.

Deborah Szekely and the Dalai Lama are right, of course. To be ageless, and to experience inner peace, we should choose to do the things that enhance our lives on the way to inner peace, and we should eliminate the things that, even if pleasurable for the short term, ultimately diminish our lives and create inner stress. The question is, why is something that seems so simple so hard for so many of us to do? And how can we accomplish it?

You can learn to lead a happier, more fulfilled life at any age. You can also grow older without growing wiser. Age doesn't necessarily bring wisdom; *evolving* brings wisdom. It's up to each of us as individuals to choose whether we will evolve and how committed we are to evolving. The commitment begins with choosing to become more mindfully aware of how you make the choices in your life, whether you're mindfully making choices about how you think and behave or letting your default programming make the choices for you on automatic pilot without you even knowing it. If you're dissatisfied with your current experience of life, it's a clue that your programming is running you, and this is your opportunity to learn to interrupt it and make healthier, more productive choices.

My purpose in writing this book is to share insights, information, and methods to help you have more pleasurable experiences that will enhance your life and lead to inner peace.

····· PART I ·····

THE PAST: AN ILLUMINATING PLACE TO VISIT, BUT YOU DON'T WANT TO LIVE THERE

CHAPTER ONE

THE VOICE IN YOUR HEAD—
AND WHY IT'S SO OFTEN WRONG

····· 🧠 ·····

Enlightenment can come only when we can transcend and silence the voice in our head. For most of us, that voice is talking to us all the time, making judgments and telling us how to act.

The first step to enlightenment occurs when you recognize that *the voice in your head is not you; it's only a part of you. It's also not your boss, and it's not necessarily accurate*; what it says *may* be accurate, but often it is wrong and just has the appearance of being "the way it is."

The voice in your head never intentionally lies to you, but what it tells you is its *interpretation* of the truth. All of its interpretations are viewed through the filter of your mind's programming. Once you learn how your mind is programmed, you'll see why the voice in your head is frequently wrong in what it tells you about a given situation—and you'll see how what it tells you may be very bad advice that actually prevents you from getting what you want.

Understanding the Way Your Mind Works

The story of Adam and Eve is a great metaphor to help us understand how our minds work. When Adam and Eve lived in the Garden of Eden they lived in a state of pure *beingness,* experiencing complete harmony, without worry, fear, or the need to protect themselves or strategize for their survival. They were *always* in the now, the present, connected to each other, to Source, to Higher Power. No value judgments or interpretations interfered with their bliss. They would have remained in that state for eternity were it not for the serpent tempting them to disobey God.

As a result of eating the forbidden fruit, Adam and Eve were thrust out of Eden and became the first mortals, and with that came the need to survive. All at once the world contained threats, and they needed a mind capable of preemptive, defensive thinking, a mind able to anticipate, to identify, and to judge everything they encountered in the outside world. This became the voice in their head as they emerged from Eden.

Adam and Eve's fearless days lounging around the pool in the Garden of Eden without a worry or care were replaced by experiencing their lives with the commentary of the often-critical voice in their head as it attempted to help them with their constant struggle for survival. From that point forward, humanity rarely experienced harmony.

As Adam and Eve's descendants, we have inherited the same kind of judging mind that scans every situation, evaluating everyone and everything as it looks for threats and tells us what to think and to feel about ourselves and the world outside us. The mind has become our central command center. When the mind is on automatic pilot, preoccupied with scanning and evaluating, I refer to it as our *machinery*, which speaks to us through the voice in our head. It's like having a constant GPS voice just like the device in our cars, except instead of telling us, "Turn left in a quarter of a mile and you will arrive at your destination," it tells us what to think and how to act and feel. The machinery that triggers the voice is still programmed to attempt to ensure your survival at any cost, whether it's telling you how you should flirt with someone you're attracted to or how to talk a traffic officer out of giving you a ticket when he just pulled you over for a rolling stop.

Generations after Adam and Eve, our cave-dwelling ancestors were hunter-gatherers living in tribes in the era of woolly mammoths. Back then, humans needed to live in tribes to survive, and they knew that being shunned by the tribe was a probable death sentence. As a result, the human mind became programmed with techniques designed to keep one's place in the tribe. Many, many millennia have passed since then, but our machinery is still programmed the same way. *We can still experience the possibility of being rejected or disapproved of by others as a matter of life and death,* and often we continue to react to those perceived threats in unnecessary ways that are inappropriate and unproductive, creating a lot of collateral damage to our relationships.

The most important words in the previous sentence are "experience . . . as a matter of life and death"; what our minds—fixated as they are on survival—may perceive momentarily as a life-and-death matter is often nothing of the sort. In the next section, I'll show you what accounts for this curious condition.

Why Being on Automatic Pilot Is Dysfunctional

To understand this common phenomenon of the mind's being so off base, remember that everything it tells you is based on its *interpretation*. The mind's interpretation of current events is based on experiences you had long ago, starting in childhood, and the way it tells you to act is based on what it believes worked in a similar situation in the past. This is how your default programming, which becomes the machinery's software, was created, and if you let it operate on automatic pilot, it will work the same way 24/7.

Automatic pilot is the opposite of being *mindfully aware*. When we are mindfully aware, we are making our decisions with thoughtful intention in the present; we are navigating our life with intention rather than simply reacting with our default programming. When we're mindfully aware, we're not being run by the voice in our head but by our being free from the judgments contained in our programming, free from allowing our machinery to control our life based on its interpretations, which may be self-defeating.

In many areas, the machinery runs things properly most of the time. For example, when your senses perceive an oncoming car, your machinery can cause you to take action that will likely save your life. But it can also mistakenly turn a simple nonissue into huge drama. For example, someone gives you what you interpret as a dirty look, and you're off to the races, ready to attack or to run away (the "fight or flight" behaviors we inherited from our cave-dwelling forebears), and the unnecessary drama takes on a life of its own.

We tend to believe that everything our machinery tells us is a fact when it isn't necessarily reporting facts. That's why it's vital to *evaluate what your mind is telling you and to make a mindfully aware choice instead of listening to a false interpretation that ultimately won't serve you.*

All kinds of pointless issues get blown out of proportion when you let your mind run you instead of you running your mind, and that is the source of self-defeating behavior. The reason I like the term *machinery* to describe the workings of the mind on autopilot is that it emphasizes that what's happening is mechanical—rote—as opposed to you making mindfully aware choices.

The difference between allowing your machinery to run you and you taking charge of making mindfully aware choices is so critical, I want to give you a few more examples to drive home its importance.

Say a friend calls to invite you to dinner. You don't really feel like going, but without even thinking you say yes. Why? Because your machinery made a snap (automatic) judgment based on "staying in the tribe" (a good tribe member would never be rude and decline a dinner invitation) instead of being mindful and looking more deeply into your feelings to see what you really feel.

Or perhaps this next example has happened to you. A friend recently said to me, "You seem angry." In the past, my old way of reacting would have been to be on automatic pilot, with no idea why she said that or whether or not I was, in fact, angry. My machinery would have interpreted the comment as unnecessary criticism and then have morphed into the interpretation that my friend was shaming and rejecting me. I would probably have gotten upset and acted defensively, denying her perception of me and attacking her.

Because today I am more present and mindfully aware, however, I recognize that being angry isn't a crime—in fact, it's sometimes a justifiable response—and that the other person's comment doesn't mean our relationship is about to end. My friend is just voicing her perception of what I was communicating at that moment. By being mindful, I can look inside to see if I am angry, and if I am, I can acknowledge it and see where the conversation goes from there.

All of us have seen that at times we have behaved inappropriately on automatic pilot. Your actions may have been inappropriate because they didn't authentically represent what you truly felt about something (as in the example of accepting an invitation when you really would rather have said no) or because your machinery misinterprets what is happening as if it's a threat (as in the example of my machinery misinterpreting a friend's comment "you seem angry" to mean that she is criticizing, shaming, and rejecting me). Today, when I act on automatic pilot in situations in which my machinery's misinterpretation leads me to behave in hurtful ways and I later reflect on my behavior, I see—and say—"It was my machinery."

I don't do this to absolve myself of responsibility—my actions are *always* my responsibility. I do this to make it clear to myself and to other people with whom I've interacted that I reacted mechanically; that I heard what I expected to hear or saw what I expected to see as a result of my mind's interpretations; that I reacted with a default response instead of reflecting on whether I heard or saw correctly so that I could respond with a mindfully aware choice.

How to Interrupt Your Machinery

To make choices with *mindful awareness*—a key concept to self-transformation that we will explore in this book—you have to be present in the moment, which means you have to *interrupt your machinery.* In other words, to just *be* in whatever situation you're in, letting go of whatever judgments and interpretations come to mind, including those about what is "good," what is "bad," what the situation "should be" (compared to what it is), and how you "should be" (compared to how you are).

Letting go of these judgments and interpretations—a major component of mindful awareness—allows you to see the facts of that situation exactly as they are and feel your own feelings exactly as they are, without judgment, without interpretation. Only then can you respond to the facts and to your actual feelings and make a mindfully aware choice about how to act.

This is why the first step toward enlightenment is recognizing that the voice in your head isn't you and that what it's telling you isn't always the truth. This recognition gives you the ability to question the voice in your head. It makes you realize that your mind's programming—with its multitude of beliefs and interpretations—*should* be questioned, that some of your most basic beliefs could be false. These include possible beliefs about yourself—for example, that you're unworthy and undeserving; about others—for example, that no one will give you what you want, so it's pointless to ask for it; and about the world—for example, that nothing ever goes your way, so why bother to strive to achieve your goals.

It may seem like a radical idea that your beliefs, which are so embedded in your programming that you've probably never questioned them, are not facts and that many may actually be wrong. In order to understand why this is so, we will look at how we unconsciously created our own programming. Before we focus on the creation of our programming, however, I want to briefly introduce you to the crucial subject of the interrelationship between your mind and your brain, which I'll discuss fully in Part II.

Your Mind and Your Brain

I once heard it said that "the mind is what the brain does for a living." I've also heard it said that "the mind's job is survival."

The meaning of "the mind's job is survival" is clear from our discussion of the way the mind scans, judges, and evaluates everything we encounter and gives us instructions to help us survive what it interprets as threats and potential threats. I've learned that "your mind is what your brain does for a living" is more than just a funny line; it's an accurate description of the way the mind and the brain interrelate, and it's why understanding how our brains work helps us understand how our minds work.

We've looked at how, because of your programming, the mind can react to something you encounter as a threat or a potential threat when in reality it's not, and we've seen that reacting as if it is can be very dysfunctional. Now let's look at how Samuel Wang, associate professor in the Department of Molecular Biology and Neuroscience at Princeton and faculty member of the Princeton Neuroscience Institute, explains how the brain functions to make dysfunctional choices.

"Popular belief has it that the brain is like a computer," Wang says. "The brain processes information, but beyond that, the analogy does not hold up well. Everyday experiences reveal ways in which your brain operates in a most uncomputer-like fashion. Examples include visual illusions, the emotional basis of decision making, irrational approaches to problem-solving, and the unreliability of human memory. These phenomena reflect the evolutionary history of the brain, which has been optimized by natural selection to help you live to fight another day and to reproduce."[1]

We can see in Wang's explanation that "visual illusions, the emotional basis of decision making, irrational approaches to problem-solving, and the unreliability of memory" are not just functions of our minds, they are functions of our brains. Although we may think of it as happening in our mind, neuroscientists have discovered that what we see, what we feel, how we decide, what we remember actually happens because of what happens in our brain, or, more properly, as you'll see in Part II, the interrelationship between the mind and the brain.

Digital technology has enabled us to see as never before the brain as we human beings use it, and the recent gains we've made in understanding our brains and the insight this gives us into ourselves is astounding. Congress declared the 1990s as "The Decade of the Brain."[2] And in 2013, President Obama announced the "BRAIN" (Brain Research through Advancing Innovative Neurotechnologies) Initiative, a plan for federal investment in brain research.[3] These are just two signs that there's been an explosion of new, often startling information about the brain as humanity approached and entered the twenty-first century. Neuroscience is the new frontier.

Discoveries about the brain are happening every day; here are just a few of them.

For years we believed that we only use 10 percent of our brain; now neuroscientists have discovered that we use all of our brain, but that at any given time certain parts of it show more activity than other parts, which doesn't mean that we aren't using them.[4]

We also used to believe that babies are born with blank slates and develop judgments only as a result of their experiences, but recent research has revealed that three-month-old babies have a sense of right and wrong. This was demonstrated in a study in which hundreds of babies were tested and showed a distinct preference for a puppet that was helpful to another puppet and a strong dislike of a puppet that hindered another puppet.[5]

Furthermore, dispelling the misconception that our brains are fully developed by late adolescence, scientists have learned that our brain isn't fully developed until we're around age twenty-five, and the last parts to mature and fully develop are those that have to do with responsible decision making and impulse control.[6] No wonder young adults often make poor decisions and engage in irresponsible behavior!

Research has also revealed that certain habits, which are formed over time and governed by the part of the brain known as the *basal ganglia*, are so powerful that even an individual who has suffered extreme brain damage can continue to perform tasks he's done many times before. For example, a brain-damaged man with little or no short-term memory can nevertheless take a walk in his neighborhood, indicating familiarity with it, even though he's unable to consciously recognize his own house or draw a map of the streets. Likewise, this man can go to the kitchen to make meals even though he can't consciously draw a floor plan of his house and indicate where the kitchen is.[7] This is *the power of habit.*

Habit is so powerful that it can lead to our persistently doing things that are self-defeating, even self-destructive. It's often been observed that one of the differences between human beings and rats is that if rats find there's no cheese at the end of a path, they stop going down that path. But we human beings often keep going down the same path even after we've found there's no cheese at the end of it. It's like the old definition of insanity: doing the same thing over and over and expecting a different result. Research on the brain has revealed why this is so: There are very specific reasons, having to do with the nature of the brain, why, when we're operating on automatic pilot, the brain will do what is familiar even if it's useless or destructive.

In other words, research on the brain has given us a clear understanding of how our default programming works *physiologically*. It has revealed the relationship between the voice in your head (that internal GPS that tells you what to think and how to act) and your brain (the organ in your skull connected to the nervous system throughout your body).

In so doing, it's revealed the connection between our individual psychology—the particular ways our experiences as individuals have influenced our mental traits—and the development of our brain. It also shows the way that our particular brain develops and then functions to influence how we think and act. Neuroscientists have discovered that our individual psychology and the physiology and functioning of our brain are inextricably tied to each other because *the experiences that have a psychological effect on us also shape our brain and influence the particular ways our brain tends to function from that time forward.*

For each person's machinery, every new experience, especially an experience that affects us significantly, is like another fork in the road, and we respond to it (consciously or unconsciously) by going down one of the roads at the fork and not another. Once this choice is made, our machinery gives us a new road map (just like the GPS system gives us new instructions after a wrong turn). Put in terms of brain science, the brain develops in such a way that it tends to keep us on the road we've chosen with "blinders"—it doesn't develop in alternative ways that lie along the road we haven't taken.

Here's an example from my childhood that should help you see how this plays out in our lives. When I was in kindergarten, we had a "rainy day afternoon" during which my teacher gave out small cartons of milk. When she gave me my carton, she told me she would open it, but I stopped her and told her I'd do it myself. While trying to open it, I spilled the milk all over her skirt, and she became very angry. Her reaction scared and humiliated me. I apologized profusely, and from that point on, I chose the road of "I'm going to do what the teacher says. Period."

As a result of that incident, my brain began developing in very specific ways (the process of which I'll explain in Part II), not only in the classroom but also in situations that felt the same, situations in which I felt that if I took a stance that conflicted with what another person wanted, he or she might become angry and humiliate me.

This kept me on the same road. The alternative road at the fork, when asserting myself as a kindergartener I accidentally spilled milk on my teacher, might have been to apologize to my teacher and to decide that, despite the embarrassment, opening the milk carton myself had still been a risk worth taking.

But this doesn't mean I was fated to go down the road of "I'm going to do what the teacher says" for the rest of my life. Nor are you fated to go down the roads that you've taken in your life up to now.

As you'll see in the chapters in Part II, brain research has revealed that our brains are malleable, with the capacity to be shaped and reshaped—scientists refer to this as the brain's *neuroplasticity*—and that however you've developed your brain before now, you can learn to use your mind to transform your brain to help you function more healthily from this point forward.[8]

Brain research has revealed what self-transformation is about on a physiological level. The malleability of your brain means that by its nature the brain makes transforming yourself possible. In fact, the research shows that *changing the way you think and act—changing your programming—by changing your brain is part of your potential as a human being, and that you can do it throughout your life!*

When you understand how your programming is formed, which is the focus in the next chapter, it will be even clearer to you why I titled this first part of the book "The Past: An Illuminating Place to Visit, but You Don't Want to Live There."

PAUSE YOUR MACHINERY

Here, and in the chapters that follow, I'll ask you to stop and take a moment to "pause your machinery." The concepts and techniques I present throughout *Your Mind Is What Your Brain Does for a Living* require mindfulness to learn and master, and these brief written exercises will give you the opportunity to rest, step outside the pattern of passive reading, and bring yourself into the present moment to reflect and see how the information I'm sharing can be integrated into your own life.

Keep your written answers, because they will be valuable for you to review later and to refer to in doing subsequent exercises. You may want to buy a notebook or open a computer file so that you can keep all of your responses together in one place.

- Take out your notebook (or open a new computer file) and describe in writing two or three recent incidents in which you now recognize that you acted or reacted the way you did because your machinery was on automatic pilot. In other words, situations about which you'd now say in reference to your behavior, "It was my machinery."
- Read over the list of incidents one at a time. Bring up the memory of each incident by pretending it's a scene in a movie being projected on the screen of your mind. Watch the scene and remember what thoughts and emotions came up for you during the action.
- See if you can identify the thoughts (interpretations, judgments) and feelings that triggered your machinery to act on automatic pilot. Write down the trigger(s) for each incident. Keep this list, because these thoughts and feelings are likely to trigger your machinery to act on automatic pilot in other situations in which they come up.

Did any negative self-thoughts come into your mind when you did this exercise? For example, in realizing that in these incidents you acted on automatic pilot, did you think that you were "wrong" or "bad" to have acted as you did? If so, recognize that this is a judgment, an interpretation, and it's part of your programming.

In each incident you've described, what happened is just what happened; *it simply is what it is.* Taking responsibility within yourself for your actions and being responsible to others doesn't mean judging or shaming yourself for them. Criticism aimed at yourself hurts you and doesn't help anyone else either. If you did judge yourself, do you think that this is part of a general pattern for you? If so, write down the kinds of judgments you habitually make about yourself. Remember to keep what you've written; it will remind you that these self-criticisms are not facts but interpretations that are part of your default programming.

Now let's look at how your programming began in childhood and can still affect your thoughts, emotions, and behaviors when you're an adult.

CHAPTER TWO

HOW PROGRAMMING FORMED IN CHILDHOOD CAN CONTROL YOU WHEN YOU'RE AN ADULT

····· 🧠 ·····

I jokingly tell people that the only person I'm aware of who has had more therapy than me is Woody Allen. When I first started therapy, I was thirty-one years old. At the time, I had no idea of my programming, let alone how it affected my relationships, nor did I realize I had played any role whatsoever in creating my own unhappiness.

I'd been married for nine years and had two daughters, yet despite deeply loving my family, I'd felt unhappy in my marriage. I moved into an apartment on my own, and my wife and I started going to a save-the-marriage therapist. I'd already become successful in business, and while I gave myself credit for my professional success, I took no responsibility for my lack of fulfillment in my marriage. I thought I was unhappy because being unhappy was the nature of life. I felt like a victim; I assumed that was just the way it was and there was nothing I could do about it.

Looking back, I can now see that the voice in my head spoke to me all the time with a running, highly judgmental and negative critique of both me and my situation. I didn't think about the voice in my head; I believed the voice *was* me. I believed that whatever it said was the truth.

The voice in my head told me I was emotionally incomplete, that somehow I was unable to understand or perhaps respond to people emotionally as other people could. I created a vivid image to explain this: All the souls were waiting in line to be outfitted with "supplies" before being born to human life, and whoever was handing out the skills for proper emotional balance was on a cigarette break when my turn came, so I didn't get any.

Up to that time, the voice in my head offered me no hope that it would ever stop being critical of me. It also offered me no hope that I could lessen the anxiety that was always with me in my personal relationships, especially in regard to potential confrontations and rejection. It never hinted to me that I wasn't a victim of life but rather a victim of my own dysfunctional programming—that I was doing the same things over and over and expecting different results!

The Moment the Baby Chick Leaves the Shell

My first glimmer that I had what I now call machinery, and that it was keeping me from really knowing myself, came early in individual therapy. When the therapist asked me about my father and my childhood, I told him everything had been "normal." When he asked me specific questions, I was shocked because I had only a few memories and had blocked everything else out. That moment of shock as I sat in the chair opposite the therapist felt as if someone had snuck the 100-plus-piece University of Southern California marching band into the room and I hadn't noticed it, even though they had been there all the time.

In the month that followed, I became aware of how much pain I was in and that I had shoved it all deep inside me, pretending there was no problem. I believed that emotional pain was par for the course—everyone had it—and therefore it was best not to pay attention to it. When I recognized I was in denial about the pain, and finally allowed myself to start feeling it, I told my therapist about a painful situation in my life and that I felt helpless to do anything about it. He responded with "It sounds like you have somebody stepping on your toe, and you don't know how to negotiate getting them off of it."

That was a moment of illumination: I realized that I felt trapped, not only in that situation but also in whatever problems I was having in my most precious relationships, because I believed that asking for my true "inner-world" needs to be met would result in other people getting so angry they would abandon me.

I'd allowed the people closest to me to step on my feet for years without ever telling them to get off because I'd never felt safe doing so. Now I was hearing the therapist tell me it was possible to ask for what I wanted; I just didn't know how to do it. As his words sank in, I was like a newborn chick poking a hole through the top of the eggshell in which it was born, seeing its first glimpse of light in the world outside the confines of its shell. A glimpse of enlightenment.

I began to sense the possibility of a world outside the confines of my own mind—the possibility of looking at my thoughts, feelings, and behavior and learning new ways of responding to situations that would be better than the ones I'd always believed were the *only* options.

In other words, for the first time, I was hearing I could learn to think and respond in ways that could get me what I instinctively craved, ways that were beyond the thoughts and responses of my default programming that was running me when I was on automatic pilot.

In the next few years I focused on gaining insights to answer the question, How did the programming that causes our automatic responses get to be the way it is? How much is nature (biology) and how much is nurture (environment)? I learned that our programming is a combination of our DNA, the genetic makeup we inherit from our parents, and environmental factors that contribute to our learned behavior. Some of it is old pre-bundled software, inherited at birth from our species's woolly mammoth days. Much of it is from our childhood experiences in the particular environment in which we were raised. This includes our interactions with our parents and others close to us as well as the messages they downloaded to us.

Our mind's machinery incorporates everything we have taken in through our five senses—seeing, hearing, touching, tasting, smelling—to create our default programming, which is constantly being updated and elaborated on, on a daily basis, for as long as we live. This programming is based on our *interpretations* of what we've experienced. Even though the process that creates our programming is the same for all of us, our programming is as individual as we are because our individual experiences and interpretations are unique to us. Indeed, it's what makes us individuals. It's as if we have all created our own individual virtual reality; we have created our own personal universe!

Growing up, I was told not to eat meat from a pig, and I didn't, but later I came to believe that "bacon doesn't count." On the other hand, as a child I had a belief that being summoned by an authority figure was a "bad thing," and it's never changed.

One of the first and most powerful times I remember experiencing this was when I was in third grade and I was called to the principal's office. I immediately became fearful that I was in trouble and would be punished. But all he wanted was to give me back a Valentine's Day lollipop that I'd brought to school for Debbi, my eight-year-old crush, and had lost before giving it to her. I thought I was in trouble but I wasn't, yet still to this day I react to a call from authority figures with default programming that makes me fearful something is wrong as opposed to responding with an expectation that I'm being called about something good! For some reason, my machinery was willing to rewrite my interpretation of bacon but not of being summoned by an authority figure.

These are minor examples of the types of judgments that get embedded in our programming, many so strongly that, like my fear of the primary school principal, they don't appear subject to change. Because we're so used to them being part of us, they just seem inevitable. Based on judgments and interpretations such as these, the voice in our head tells us stories over and over again, and these stories become the basis of our programming, which forms the patterns of our behavior.

From early childhood on, the machinery uses this programming to respond over and over to what happens in the present. These responses are very predictable, with the exception that every now and then, for no apparent reason, the machinery will react differently. This is one of the things that make us so interesting: We react to a given situation the same way over and over again and then—suddenly, inexplicably—in the same situation, we react in another way. When this happens, we may comment to ourselves that we've changed, but later we find that we go back to our old patterns. This is part of being human: We're predictable, except when we're not! But one thing that is consistently predictable is that when we're run by our default programming, most of the time we will respond in the same ways.

What Happens When Childhood Hurts Are Not Resolved

As I've said, in addition to our genetic makeup, the emotionally impactful experiences we have growing up and our reactions to those experiences are a major factor in creating our programming. We come into the world with the potential for full self-expression, able to speak and to act without censoring ourselves. But events happen that we experience as traumas, and we start suppressing our self-expression.

The word *trauma* may make you think of major catastrophic events such as an earthquake or a tsunami or a terrible accident. But a trauma can be any event that is intensely disturbing or shocking and that leaves an emotional wound—often invisible to the naked eye. It doesn't necessarily need to be a big event; a person watching it might see it as small, even inconsequential. What makes it a trauma is that it *feels* so intensely disturbing to the person experiencing it. In childhood, your reactions to events that you experience as traumatic create programming that, if you let your machinery run you on automatic pilot, will determine your behavior in response to events in the present that your conscious or unconscious mind categorizes as similar to the earlier traumatic events.

While the traumas that contribute to our programming differ, they share a common dynamic: An event occurs and our minds interpret the event to mean that *something is wrong*; then our minds draw a lesson from it about how we should act in the future, and the lesson becomes part of our programming.

For example, as an eight-year-old I was playing in the sandpit beneath the trapeze rings at the park next to our house. Older kids were swinging on the set of high rings, and two of them lifted me up to try it too. I fell off and it knocked the wind out of me; I thought I was going to die. Someone gave me artificial respiration as best he could, and once again my lungs filled with air and I was safe. I ran home, wanting to be comforted by my mom and dad yet filled with fear that if I told my parents, I would get into horrible trouble. I felt blamed, ashamed, and scared even though that was only my *perception* of what would happen.

Without knowing it, my preprogrammed machinery had kicked in. I was back in the Woolly Mammoth Age, afraid that my dad, leader of my hunting pack, would be so mad that he would yell at and punish me. My unconscious interpretation was, "You'll be out of the tribe!"—a potential death sentence.

The most common childhood traumas, according to Los Angeles psychologist Robin L. Kay, Ph.D., are ruptures of a significant emotional attachment. In the incident I just described, I assumed my father and mother would be furious that, as my child's mind saw it, I had almost died, so I couldn't even trust telling them how scared I was. This made me feel very distant from my parents, unable to communicate with them about something important and disturbing—traumatic—to me.

The bond between you and your parents is generally the most vital attachment in your childhood; you need your parents' love to feel safe. Consequently, if you experience a rupture in that attachment, it's traumatic, even if that rupture is a result of your perception of a situation. The traumatic nature of a rupture in a childhood attachment is more obvious if the incident involves your parent yelling at, neglecting, hitting, or in some other way abusing you.

Prior to the time the incident in the sandpit occurred, there had been incidents in which my father had gotten very angry and yelled at me, and these experiences had triggered my fear that he would yell at and punish me the day I fell off the rings. The earlier experiences had set me on the road to avoiding his anger at all costs. The message that had entered my programming based on my interpretation of these incidents was, "You better be super good and never do anything wrong so that no one will be angry at you and you'll be safe!" (The incidents that included my father yelling at me also probably contributed to my fear of the principal and authority figures in general.)

Kay says that a parent, an older sibling, a neighbor, or someone else close to a child can repair a rupture in real time, soon after the event, by helping the child to process the reality of the event and the emotions associated with it. And according to some mental health professionals, in order for "good enough" development of a child to take place—meaning that the child will have a generally positive self-image, function well in the world, and act in ways that are conducive to achieving his or her goals—only 50 percent of attachment ruptures need to be repaired. The fewer times someone helps you to repair traumas when you're a child, the more negative programming you have as an adult.

Let's look at an example of how a parent can repair a rupture in his or her child's attachment. When I was five years old, my father walked into the living room, found me drawing in his high school yearbook, and yelled at me. I became frightened and upset. My father grabbed his yearbook and left me in the living room, crying. I loved my father very much, and I believed he was punishing me with rejection for drawing in the book. In order to repair the rupture, my father could have calmed himself down, come back a few minutes later, and hugged and comforted me. He could have told me he loved me and he hadn't meant to get so angry at me. He could have said I was a good kid and that I was doing what good kids do, drawing and entertaining myself. He could have told me he realized that I didn't know I shouldn't draw in his special yearbook.

The problem is that it never occurred to my father to notice my distress and explain the situation to me; he probably handled it in the same way his father had treated him. Like many parents, my father didn't know how to heal the ruptured attachment and how important it is for parents to do so, and so he didn't do it. This event, in which the ruptured attachment wasn't resolved, occurred three years before the playground incident I described and was one of the reasons that, much as I needed comforting then, I was afraid to go to my father and mother after I'd fallen and had the wind knocked out of me.

Starting in the 1950s, psychologist Harry Harlow performed experiments with rhesus monkeys in order to study attachment between mother and baby during infancy. He removed the monkeys from their mothers shortly after birth and gave them surrogate mothers that provided them with milk. Some "mothers" were made of wire mesh and others were covered with foam and soft cloth. Both types of surrogate mothers had electric lights inside them that made them warm.

The monkeys that had wire surrogate mothers soon exhibited behavior, such as rocking, that showed they were distressed, and they also exhibited antisocial behavior. The monkeys that had cloth-and-foam-covered mothers didn't exhibit distress or any antisocial behavior. Harlow's experiment showed that food and warmth alone aren't sufficient for baby monkeys to become emotionally healthy; affection and closeness (simulated in the experiment by the foam and softer covering, as well as the warmth of the electric light) are also necessary.

Because of the rhesus monkeys' similarity to human beings, Harlow applied these findings to human babies, concluding that they, too, need their caregiver's love, affection, and acceptance in addition to food, warmth, and safety. His findings contributed a great deal to our understanding of the bond between mother and child and the psychological and physical effects, which can continue into adulthood, that result from a caregiver's insufficiently meeting a baby's needs.[1]

I think of parents who, because of their own biology or DNA or childhood environment or unresolved traumas—or a combination of these factors—aren't capable of repairing ruptures with their children at least 50 percent of the time, as "wire monkey parents." If one or both of your parents was a wire monkey parent, you're going to have had more unrepaired ruptures in your childhood, and your responses to these unrepaired ruptures will have had a major impact on your programming.

By definition, these unrepaired ruptures involve emotional pain. Other emotions, all of which are built on the basic emotions of love, anger, grief, and guilt, quickly become layered on top of the pain. When the trauma remains unrepaired, these emotions remain with you, but you may not be aware of them. Often you repress them with defenses, which blocks you from fully experiencing them because your conscious mind finds them unacceptable. Not only do these unrepaired traumas become part of your programming, so do the emotions layered on top of them and the beliefs you draw from your interpretations of the traumas. These elements of your past, embedded in your programming, contribute to dysfunctional behavior in the present.

PAUSE YOUR MACHINERY

- Reflect on your childhood to see if you remember any events in which your emotional bond with your mother or father (or someone else close to you) was ruptured in a way that felt traumatic to you at the time, or that you now see as traumatic. If you remember one or more such events, write a description of what happened in each and how you recall feeling at the time. It may help you to think about where you were when the incident happened, what you were wearing, or if there is a particular smell or taste that you associate with the experience. Bring to mind as much as you can from that time. Also write down how you feel about it now and what thoughts occur to you as you look back on it.

- Write down whether you feel that the rupture was repaired or if it was left unrepaired (or unresolved).

- Write down your thoughts about whether your parents or others close to you were generally able or unable to repair ruptures that occurred. Please keep in mind that you may have the possibility of repairing these ruptures today if you use the information and tools you'll learn in this book.

As you've seen, the unresolved emotional pain we experienced in childhood has a profound effect on our default programming. In the next chapter, I'll discuss how it contributes to our conscious and unconscious beliefs about ourselves and the emotions we experience in our daily lives.

CHAPTER THREE

YOUR CONSCIOUS
AND UNCONSCIOUS BELIEFS

..... 🧠 .....

Our beliefs are both a cause and a result of our fundamental programming. The specific beliefs we develop are based on our childhood experiences, and our mind's interpretations of those experiences, so they vary for each of us, but they all contain some form of the following judgments about ourselves and our place in the world:

- Something is wrong.
- I'm not good enough.
- I don't belong here.
- I'm always going to be on my own.

It's almost impossible for children to avoid these thought forms as they grow up. It's part of the way our machinery works in childhood and will continue to work until we learn to interrupt it. This kind of negative programming doesn't help us in situations in which we feel frustration, anxiety, and stress. Indeed, it *causes* frustration, anxiety, and stress.

At this point, you might be wondering why your machinery, which is set up to help you *survive*, contains aspects within its programming that create in you these states of being upset and get in the way of you reaching your goals. The answer goes back to the fact that the programming on which our machinery bases its actions is composed of relics of past-based interpretations that are often incorrect.

When my eyes scan the street as I'm about to step into it and I see a car coming, the voice in my head tells me to wait until the car passes. This interpretation is accurate and works for my survival. But when someone says to me, "Steve, you're wrong; you don't understand what I was saying," my machinery interprets it as if he's saying I'm stupid or incompetent. In reality he may not be criticizing me or putting me down; he may just be telling me that he's saying something that's important to him and he wants me to understand it more accurately. Because of my machinery's interpretation, though, I become defensive or go on the attack, which would be inappropriate and dysfunctional since with either behavior I would be creating bad feelings and distance instead of closeness in my relationship with the other person.

A cardinal principle for us to understand is that, in general, the machinery hears and sees what it expects to hear and see and we believe that what we're seeing and hearing is accurate, even though the "sender" may be intending an entirely different message.

Such misinterpretations often result in our machinery's getting *activated*—going on full battle alert—which makes us respond as if our life is being threatened, whether that threat is real or imagined.

Why would my machinery react this way simply because someone said I didn't understand what he was saying? Because my default programming tells me that I have to be 100 percent right all the time or I'm in trouble. With this belief in my programming, my machinery is always on the lookout for any comment that could mean I'm less than 100 percent right, and my old way of responding to a perceived threat was to become either defensive or aggressive.

The instant my machinery interprets an incoming experience as criticism, even if it's just a look that's interpreted as implying that I'm less than 100 percent right, my machinery's first reaction is to trigger feelings of shame and blame. The perceived shame or blame brings me right back to being a child summoned to the principal's office. All four of the beliefs I listed in the opening of this chapter—*something is wrong; I'm not good enough; I don't belong here;* and *I'm always going to be on my own*—take their place, front and center, in my activated machinery.

My sense of self-worth temporarily goes on "tilt." My inner world hates seeing me like this; it's too painful. My machinery is telling me that I have no choice but to vindicate myself. To protect myself from the perceived threat, I start using old tapes: *automatics,* which means I'm *reacting,* that is, responding and acting on automatic pilot, using a repertoire of strategies from earlier in my life that my mind judged to have been the best tools for handling past situations. Since at the moment I'm on automatic pilot, my mind applies these strategies—getting defensive or going on the attack—even if they really *didn't* work before and *don't* apply to the current situation. It does this because, on automatic pilot, our mind doesn't judge these strategies objectively; it judges them with the interpretations in our programming.

Until you become aware of your machinery's programming and learn to interrupt it, you're likely to keep doing the same things over and over, always creating the same results even though you might like and benefit from a different approach. It goes back to the old definition of insanity: repeating the same behavior over and over and expecting a different result. This will happen as long as you let your machinery take the controls and sabotage you.

Remember: When the machinery is activated, taking charge and giving commands about how to respond to a perceived threat, it kidnaps you and takes you out of the present. Only through mindful awareness can you experience what is actually occurring in the present. Being reactive because your machinery has been activated is the opposite of being mindfully aware.

What Feelings Does Your Machinery Activate When It's on Autopilot?

Up to this point, I've explained the links between past events, your mind's interpretations of them, and the ways in which your automatic pilot's programming uses these interpretations to cause your actions and reactions in the present. It's important to recognize that the voice in your head doesn't necessarily explain the chain of interpretations that the mind uses to connect what happened in the past to what's happening in a current situation; often it just cues you to act or react without going through a thought process about *why*.

But although you may not experience a thought process linking the present to the past, in an activated state you probably will experience *feelings*. Among these—whether individually or in combination—are anger, fear, joy, sadness, love, affection, grief, and guilt. You may experience an internal conflict between opposite emotions and points of view about what you should do, making you feel trapped, fearful that there's no way out of the situation.

You may be in a heightened state of "fight or flight" or "engage or disengage" or you may even go numb as your machinery chooses its tools to protect you. In this state, your emotions often become exaggerated and distorted, and you may become anxious. You might not even be aware of what's going on emotionally; you may simply just feel *bad*. There is generally a *tone of feeling* that puts a filter on everything. This is where the saying "When dad has a bad day at work, the dog gets kicked" comes from.

Our machinery is filled with defenses: unconscious strategies, including denial, that operate automatically in order to protect our idea of ourselves by blocking thoughts and feelings that would conflict with our self-image. These defenses cause us not to see or feel what is actually going on, and to repress many feelings without a clue that we're repressing them. When our programming judges feelings to be too dangerous for us to handle, our minds automatically hide them in our unconscious and damp them down. The result is we have no awareness of them, and all we feel is anxiety. I've learned that one of my reactions to anxiety is to hold my breath without even realizing I'm doing it. The act of holding my breath just intensifies the anxiety.

The crucial point is that when your machinery is in the driver's seat, the feelings you're feeling are generally not in response to what's actually happening in the present; whatever you're feeling is determined by your programming's interpreting the current situation through the filter of its interpretations of past experiences. Just because a feeling is intense doesn't mean it's in response to the present. Often, in fact, the high intensity of a feeling is a clue that you're responding not to the present situation but to your programming's judging the present situation to be similar to a past trauma.

When we learn to interrupt our machinery and become aware of our programming and its interpretations, we can make mindful choices so that our feelings, instead of being programmed automatically, will be appropriate "feeling responses" to the present.

When we are fully present, we experience a connection to Self, to the full range of true feelings; we are capable of being at peace; we can experience a connectedness to Higher Power. When we are fully present, I think of it as being the Self with a capital "S"—in contrast to the self with a small "s" (i.e., the "I" and "me" that we think of as ourselves but are actually our machinery's perception of ourselves, often referred to as the *ego*).

When I began individual therapy, my perception of myself was still my machinery's perception. The problems that I brought up with my therapist were what I call "pebbles in the shoe," small daily issues that I found annoying or irritating and, most of all, seem to have had priority over all other thoughts. At the beginning, I didn't yet know it was possible to understand my feelings and thought processes. But the questions my therapist posed probed my inner world and started to shed light on how my internal psychological issues and the way my mind worked on automatic pilot were determining my experience of life. Until then, I'd never realized that not only were my inner-world issues hidden from others, I'd also hidden them from myself.

Becoming more aware of what caused me to act and react as I did was like waking up from sleepwalking. I started to see patterns to my behavior, often with specific triggers, and that these patterns were related to coping strategies I'd unconsciously developed over the years to deal with—actually to avoid—my feelings.

I learned that these coping strategies frequently caused problems and made the problems linger, creating frustration and stress in my relationships. I was always saying I wanted intimacy and fulfillment in my relationships, but my actions with the people closest to me were often the precise behaviors that would rob me of the intimacy and fulfillment I longed for.

I think of a good therapist as a guide who can take you through your inner world like a docent in a museum takes you on a tour of paintings and explains things that are there to see but that you don't have the practiced eye to detect yourself. I was once in a museum looking at the works of El Greco, for instance. The docent pointed out that the self-portrait we were looking at was what the artist saw in the mirror, which immediately shifted my perception of the painting. I could have figured that out, but until the docent commented on it, it never occurred to me to look at the portrait from that particular point of view. A good therapist is like a docent of our minds and emotions, asking questions that we're not asking ourselves, allowing us to notice our thoughts and feelings in a different way, from another point of view.

Through therapy, I started to become aware of my machinery and its programming by recognizing my core issues: the traumas I'd experienced in childhood and the interpretations and emotions that my mind had layered on top of the actual events. I began to see that I could start making mindful choices instead of reacting automatically. For the first time, I could see that it was possible to create a new kind of movement in my life instead of staying stuck in the same place.

As you've seen, our programming contains interpretations of events from our past. This includes every story we've ever told ourselves about ourselves (some of which we may not even consciously remember), the world around us, the people in our lives, and the circumstances, even the objects, we encounter. Until we become mindful observers of our own inner world, we don't recognize that these are just stories we've made up, just our own projections, perceived through our own filters. We believe these stories are true and, until we become mindful, don't realize it's not necessary for us to be trapped by them. Once we recognize this, we see that we have choices about how we can act in the present, and we are free for the first time!

PAUSE YOUR MACHINERY

- Review the four basic beliefs that are common in default programming:
  - Something is wrong.
  - I'm not good enough.
  - I don't belong here.
  - I'm always going to be on my own.
- In various situations, do you find yourself recurrently feeling that one or more of these beliefs are true for you? If so, write

down the belief (or beliefs) that you identify with. When this belief comes into your mind, is it phrased the way it is above or does your mind have another way of phrasing it as it tells you it applies to you? (For example, instead of "I'm not good enough," does the voice in your head indicate a particular way that you're "not good enough," such as "I'm not likeable enough," "I'm not attractive enough," or "I'm not smart enough"?) If so, write down the variation(s) of the belief. Remember to keep this list, along with your list of judgments from the exercise in Chapter 1, as they will remind you of the negative self-judgments that are contained in your default programming.

- Think back over the last week and see if there are any times that you felt shamed and/or blamed and reacted with your machinery on automatic pilot. If you can remember one or more such incidents, write a description of each, including what triggered your machinery to activate you feeling that way and to respond as you did. For example, what did another person say that made you feel as if he or she was shaming and/or blaming you? Reflecting on it now, do you think that in reality the other person was trying to shame and/or blame you or was it your interpretation of what he or she said?

- If it was your interpretation, write down the difference between what was actually said and how you heard and interpreted it. Write down how your interpretation made you feel—the emotions that were stirred up—and whether you were activated to go on the defensive or activated to become passive and to withdraw. Then write down how you would respond to the situation mindfully.

- If the other person was actually attempting to shame and/or blame you, write down how you would respond to the situation mindfully and contrast it with how you reacted from your machinery.

In the next chapter, we'll take a closer look at how the traumas we experience as children, and the lessons we draw from them, shape our programming. I'll show you how this process works by using as an example the core events, issues, and interpretations that shaped my programming. This will lay the groundwork for looking at the way your brain works and the process of freeing yourself from being run by your default programming.

CHAPTER FOUR

HOW CHILDHOOD TRAUMAS INFLUENCE YOUR PROGRAMMING

..... 🧠 .....

I've noticed that many of us have a single story or trauma from our childhood that both creates and defines the filter through which we see much of the world and that has had a tremendous impact on our path since childhood. The major event in my childhood that influenced my future programming was my father's sudden death from a cerebral hemorrhage when he was thirty-eight years old and I was eleven.

We lived in a tiny two-bedroom house. I was awakened in the middle of the night by a strange groaning that turned out to be from my father. I went to my parents' bedroom, where my mom was hysterical. A little while later, I saw my father on a stretcher being loaded into an ambulance. My mother climbed in with him, and the ambulance pulled away. I was left alone in the house with my brother, who was three years older. A few hours later our mother came back, clutching our father's underwear and screaming hysterically, "He's dead!"

Up to that time, my home life had already been emotionally chaotic, and in that world my father had seemed to be the only focused, dependable person and therefore the only one I could rely on. My older brother had been introverted and often difficult for the family to deal with. My parents were always mad and upset at him. My mother was exceptionally fearful and frequently emotionally explosive as well, with a flair for drama and hysteria. She and my father often fought. My father's presence had been reassuring; to me, he had seemed strong and capable. And, despite his occasionally being upset with me—which I avoided as much as possible—I never feared that he'd go out of control the way my mother did. I wanted to avoid both Mom and Dad getting mad at me no matter the cost. My childhood mind decided that if I was "super good," no one would be angry with me and I'd be safe.

I've mentioned that the machinery always works the same way over and over again—except when it doesn't. Not only are our actions sometimes inconsistent, our programming can contain inconsistencies too. One of my programming's inconsistencies was that even though a major part of it had the goal of making me "super good," no one, regardless of what they said, could stop me from doing what I wanted if I thought it was right.

Let me describe an incident that illustrates my determination. I was five and had just gotten a new state-of-the-art portable radio, which in those days was the size of a toaster. It came with a leather case and a shoulder strap. We were on a family outing in our car, driving along the highway, when I noticed that my radio's shoulder strap had gotten caught in the car door. I asked my father to stop the car but he wouldn't, so I opened the door to free the strap anyway.

The car had what they called "suicide doors" that caught the wind if opened when the car was moving. I was flung out into the middle of the highway. It was a huge drama. I should have been killed but I survived with only scrapes and bruises, and my interpretation was that I was almost invincible. My *will* was unstoppable! This became part of my default programming.

Another significant interpretation embedded in my child's programming came from being told and believing that anger was wrong or "bad." As part of my mission to be super good and not do anything wrong, my mind drew the conclusion that I should never be angry. I saw what my brother's anger did to both him and the family, and I wasn't willing to ever take that chance. I just swallowed my anger and any other feelings that I thought might get me into trouble.

Another factor that contributed to my developing programming that caused me to swallow my feelings came from what I observed about my mother's relationships with her family and my father's family. I'd seen her cut people out of her life when they'd had disagreements with her, and I adopted the belief that I shouldn't disagree with anyone important to me. Instead, I should find a way to mollify and give them what they wanted. My interpretation was that if you disagreed with someone, he or she would cut you out and you'd be alone. Given this belief, it became especially important to me to comply with what the people closest to me—the people I was most dependent on—requested, even if it was at my emotional expense.

Thus, even before the trauma of losing my father, I was on a very narrow emotional tightrope, stuck in the role of the "good boy," giving people what they wanted, always appearing to be happy, hiding my unhappiness—even from myself—and never being angry. (At least that's what I thought I was feeling and projecting.)

All of this was aimed at keeping myself from being abandoned.

Then my father died. I lost the only person in my world who I believed could protect me. The rupture in the bond between my father and me was now real and permanent: He was dead; he abandoned me.

Two days later, at the funeral, in keeping with the Jewish tradition, the rabbi cut my tie in half to expose my heart and to symbolize my grief for the loss of my parent, and I formally entered the fatherless phase of my life. Lots of people came to our tiny house after the funeral. I had no idea who most of them were, and I felt they were treating me with pity, which made me cringe inside.

Upset and scared, I needed my mother, but I couldn't find her. Finally, I discovered her in our garage, crying hysterically and almost chanting, "I want to die!" My eleven-year-old machinery went into survival mode: If she committed suicide, I'd be an orphan and would have no one at all. The involuntary words shot from my mouth: "Don't worry, Mom, I'll take care of you!" (I'd seen children in the movies of the day saying the same thing, so I said it to her.)

That vow to my mother in the garage became my way of life from then on. I began living my life with a new, overwhelming sense of responsibility. The new interpretation that went into my programming was: "It's all up to me!" Without knowing it, I became a *parentified child*, the term used in the therapeutic community to mean a child whose role is reversed so that he or she feels the necessity of taking charge of a parent instead of vice versa.

My child's sense of commitment made me feel that I could handle anything that came along, and as each year passed, I became more proficient at it until I became masterful! I took care of my mother when she was emotionally low and reassured her that everything was okay. When I was thirteen, I started making money selling magazines door-to-door, somehow thinking that would help and committing myself, in my mind, to continue making money to support the family. More than anything, I took care of myself so that I would never be a burden on her.

When I was eighteen, my mother was in a fragile emotional state (she didn't trust herself and feared she would be swindled by a man in her life), so she placed all the family assets in a non-revocable trust and named me as the trustee. Seven years after my father's death, I became the official financial leader of our family of three.

This programming silently ran my life and I didn't have a clue it was running me or why I felt that to survive I *had* to do *everything*: for myself, for my mother, for my brother, and, later, for my wife and my children. I believed it was my job to take care of everything, which included making the people closest to me happy and never expecting or even asking them to take care of me. Without consciously knowing this, I felt great pressure to please and take care of all of them because I feared that if I didn't please them, they would cut me off. I also needed to take care of them because I didn't believe they could take care of themselves as well as I could.

My machinery was quick to scold me when I didn't live up to my image of being all things to all people. If anyone close to me criticized me, outwardly I would automatically defend myself, but my self-critic would join in the criticism, and inwardly I would beat myself up. That critical voice took the form of echoing the four beliefs I described in Chapter 3: *something is wrong; I'm not good enough; I don't belong here;* and *I'm always going to be on my own.* I'd cast myself as being totally responsible for everyone and for pleasing everyone, and I had no idea that I hated it. My machinery hid my anger from my conscious mind. It wasn't until I was in therapy many years later that I learned how much anger and rage were inside me.

The Feelings You Don't Acknowledge Can Control You

I rarely shared with anyone what my family situation had been during my childhood and adolescence. When people asked about my childhood, I honestly told them—just as I told the therapist when he first asked me—that I'd had a "regular" childhood, and I never talked about the problems I experienced. I not only didn't talk about these problems with others, I also didn't like thinking about them myself, and I didn't. I had hated feeling pitied after my father died, and I vowed to myself that I'd never give anyone any reason to pity me.

I didn't realize that I had unconsciously cut myself off from my own empathy for myself. I had little or no effective ability to know and experience my own feelings, let alone to nurture myself. I didn't realize that the beliefs embedded in my programming—that I had to do everything on my own and that no one could stop me—were handicapping me in my personal relationships even while they were contributing to my financial success through business.

Gradually, I began to see the core events from my childhood with a new understanding that put me on a path to recognizing how they had shaped my life. I began to have an inkling of the anger and resentment I was hiding from myself. I started, through therapy, to become dimly aware that suppressing those feelings was keeping me stuck in the past, killing off much of the joy I could potentially find in my closest relationships. I began to see how hard I worked just to try to feel okay about myself, and how I had trapped myself by disallowing myself the right of full self-expression out of fear that it would cause the people closest to me to abandon me. Close as they were, I wasn't able to tell them, or even to realize, that they were stepping on my toes and I wasn't able to negotiate getting them off.

I started to realize that my drive for success in the world was fueled by my need to look worthy in the eyes of others, which I hoped would make me see myself as worthy in my own eyes.

To the outside world, I was outgoing, witty, accomplished, and apparently content. Internally, and often to the people closest to me, however, I was still very much the little fatherless boy who was overwhelmed by the responsibility of taking care of everyone and was committed to denying that he was angry because of it.

I had no idea that the pain I was not aware of was running me. Denial is one of the strongest defenses we use to block feelings, especially painful ones that our mind judges to be unacceptable to us and to others. My machinery found painful feelings dangerous. Every time pain shows up, my machinery creates the side effect of anxiety as a camouflage to mask the pain. My machinery couldn't tolerate my true feelings; as a result, without being aware of it, I cut them off and sent them to my unconscious. Even after being exposed to these explanations through therapy and growing to understand my programming and machinery, I continued cutting myself off from my true feelings at the cost of closeness in my dearest relationships. I divorced at thirty-one and remarried at thirty-six, but my core conflicts were still feeding my machinery's denial mechanisms.

Here's the way my programming to deny pain works against me in relationships: Because of my childhood issues surrounding pain, loss, and abandonment, a primary goal of my programming is for me not to experience pain, or even upsets, in my relationships. Since this programming is based on my fear of potential pain—being hurt or abandoned or both—when my machinery is on automatic pilot, its mission is to help me avoid feeling pain, even though one of the side effects of this is that I can't be fully present in close relationships or even close to myself. As a result, although I've longed for closeness since childhood, when my machinery is running me, it makes me far less emotionally available—in other words, far more unreachable—supposedly so that I won't be hurt. This makes closeness very difficult.

I had no clue that I was operating this way. Even when I took the chance and got close to someone, my machinery frequently persisted in testing that closeness: I would do or say things to push the other person's buttons to see if she would stay close to me anyway. This was, essentially, just another way of pushing people away.

Our machinery is as much a part of us as our skin and it will never go away; our old default programming will continue to echo in our head long after we've become aware of it. This means that even though I'm aware of how my machinery operates, with its programming to avoid anticipated pain, I still have to commit to using mindful awareness to fight against this tendency, to make sure my programming doesn't take the driver's seat and keep me in the past rather than allowing me to be in the present.

Here are two vital points I've learned:

1. When you're in denial about your pain, about your deepest wounds, the pain you're in denial about affects your relationships anyway.

2. Becoming aware of your machinery and its programming isn't enough. In order to live in the present, you have to interrupt your machinery, mindfully observe your programming without judgment, and make an intentional choice to respond to the present situation in an appropriate way that recognizes the facts of the situation without interpretation and that is in harmony with your true feelings.

Remember: The present is where potential and possibility live, not in the past or in the future. Your automatic pre-programmed responses are based in the past, and they block your ability to be in the present. So if you let yourself be controlled by the past, you will never be in the present; you'll just repeat the past and turn your future into your past, where there is no potential, no possibility for something new.

PAUSE YOUR MACHINERY

- Think mindfully about how you might still be controlled by traumatic experiences in your past. Remember, traumas can be both big and small events. Some of the big traumatic events are when a parent or someone else very close to you dies or disappears from your life in some other way, or when parents divorce, or they may be experiences of emotional, physical, or sexual abuse. Some of the smaller traumatic events are living with a volatile or highly critical parent, which can create daily attachment ruptures for children. (And as we saw in Chapter 2, if left unrepaired such ruptures are traumatic.)

- List any traumatic experiences from your past that you think are embedded in your programming and are running you when you're on automatic pilot. (As a starting point, refer to the list of ruptures that you wrote about in response to the Pause Your Machinery exercise at the end of Chapter 2.)

- What interpretations and judgments about yourself, other people, and the world do you think you drew from these traumas? Remember, these interpretations and judgments are also embedded in your programming. Describe them.

- Think mindfully about and describe how these interpretations and judgments from the past are influencing how you think, act, and react today. Consider how freeing it would be if you could eliminate or even reduce the power that they have over the way you think and live today.

I've mentioned that in recent decades neuroscientists have made immense advances in learning about the brain. In Part II, we'll look at how these discoveries add a dimension to our understanding of our default programming and the process of self-transformation.

THE MIND AND THE BRAIN:

WHY YOUR MACHINERY

WORKS THE WAY IT DOES

AND HOW YOUR BRAIN

ALLOWS YOU TO CHANGE

CHAPTER FIVE

WHAT YOU NEED TO KNOW ABOUT YOUR BRAIN AND HOW IT INFLUENCES THE WAY YOU ACT

..... 🧠 .....

Up to now you've seen the way your programming is formed and how, by being mindfully aware, you can learn to identify the experiences that shaped that programming. You've also learned that you can interrupt your machinery so you stop running on automatic pilot, and in so doing you can make mindful choices to think and act in healthier, more productive ways that will help you to fulfill your goals.

Now I'm going to share what I've learned about how our brains work and why, from the perspective of how the brain develops and functions, we tend to repeat past behavior. I'll also share with you *why* you have the power to transform yourself and change your thinking and behavior to create a more harmonious, fulfilling life.

In high school we learned that the brain is an organ in our head made up of *neurons* (nerve cells), which controls voluntary and involuntary actions and gives us the ability to think. Technological breakthroughs in the Digital Age have resulted in incredible knowledge about the physiology of the brain, how it works, and the relationship between the mind and the brain.

Many of these new findings have been a revelation. They increase our understanding of the way the mind operates, that is, the biological basis for how the machinery works and how it is programmed. They explain why the past continues to exert such a strong influence on us, especially when we are on automatic pilot. Most importantly, what scientists have learned about the brain shows that *when we commit to using our mind to change dysfunctional programming, we are actually changing the brain to operate in a healthier way.* These findings are inspiring. They tell us about our ability to transform ourselves—how we can develop a greater sense of well-being and learn to act in new ways that will help us achieve our goals, including having more fulfillment in our relationships. Most valuably of all, they provide a road map for making these changes any time throughout our lives!

Before looking at how the brain works and what the biology of the brain tells us about our capacity to change, it's helpful to know a few basics about the brain's structure and about the areas of behavior that each part governs.

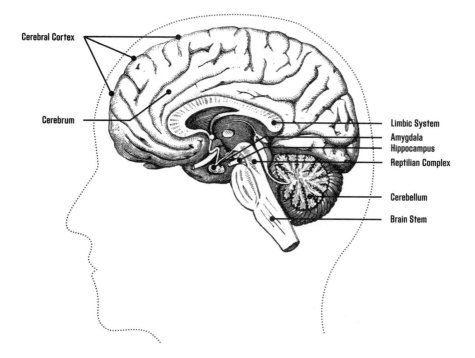

The brain is made up of three layers that developed at different times during our species' history to handle successive evolutionary needs.[1] The first and oldest layer of the brain is the *reptilian complex*, which contains the brain stem and the cerebellum; it functions for our physical survival, regulating digestion, reproduction, circulation, breathing, and the "fight or flight" response. The reptilian complex governs survival behaviors that cause us to act automatically, and the behaviors it activates strongly resist change.[2]

The second oldest part of the brain is the *limbic system*, which contains the brain's major emotional centers. One of its primary components is the *amygdala*, the part of the brain that associates events with emotions. The amygdala is the fear center, and it becomes activated whenever you are in a situation that you perceive as a threat. The amygdala is also associated with memory and with situations that, in addition to fear, give rise to emotions such as anger, indignation, rage, and pity. Another part of the limbic system, the *hippocampus,* takes in information from the present and processes it into long-term memory and is involved with recalling memories. The limbic system also participates in responses relating to sex and food, especially those associated with smell and with emotions associated with bonding and attachment.[3]

The most recent part of the brain to develop is the *cortex.* Making up five-sixths of your brain, the cortex is the outer part of the brain and is responsible for the higher-function cognitive capabilities of language, logic, and planning. One area in the cortex involves voluntary movement and another area processes sensory information.[4] With its language, logic, and planning abilities, the cortex is the part of your brain that allows you to be mindfully aware, to observe your own thinking and reflect on it. It's the cortex that allows you to identify dysfunctional programming, to stop yourself from acting on automatic pilot, and instead to make healthy choices that will help you achieve your goals and increase your sense of well-being.

When you are on automatic pilot, you are under the control of the primitive responses of the reptilian brain and the emotional responses of the limbic system. The reason it's possible to act mindfully instead of on automatic pilot is that the three layers of the brain interact all the time through the neurons that connect them to each other. This means that while one part of your brain may tend to dominate in a given situation, it is still associated with and influenced by the other parts.[5]

So, as you learn to become more mindful, your cerebral cortex, with its higher functions of language, logic, and planning, can influence and modulate the emotional responses of the limbic system and the survival responses of the reptilian complex. Because the brain is also connected to the nervous system throughout the body, as you become more mindful your cerebral cortex also improves in its ability to pick up signals from the rest of your body and to regulate your body to promote physical health.[6]

To put this into the terms I used in Part I, the process of self-transformation is the process of using the higher functions of your cerebral cortex to enable you to be in the present, and to prevent you from acting on your programming's misinterpretations of events as threats to your survival. This advanced functioning short-circuits inappropriate emotional responses that the machinery triggers and allows you instead to act in appropriate ways based on what is actually occurring in the moment. This transforms behavior in the moment and, over time, allows you to transform your brain's ability to communicate with your own body so that it functions in a healthier way.

What Brain Science Teaches You about Healing Yourself

I first learned about the structure and function of the brain and their connection to how we think and behave when I was in therapy with Ron Levine, Ph.D., who introduced me to *The Little Book of Big Stuff About the Brain: The True Story of Your Amazing Brain* by British pediatric neurologist Andrew Curran. What I refer to as dysfunctional programming Curran discusses in terms of *emotional intelligence,* or, to be more precise, a lack of it. Emotional intelligence, a concept popularized by Daniel Goleman, Ph.D., in his bestseller *Emotional Intelligence: Why It Can Matter More Than IQ,* is defined by Curran as "the ability to be aware of your own and other people's feelings." Curran stresses that emotional intelligence is vital for conducting ourselves successfully in the world.[7]

As Curran puts it, knowing "how your brain structurally contains and controls behavior . . . can help you heal yourself."[8] As you'll see, understanding the relationship between how your brain works and how you act throws light on what happens when you're acting on automatic pilot, with a lack of emotional intelligence, as well as what happens when you act mindfully.

Let's start with the amygdala, which is part of the limbic system and is the brain's fear center. The amygdala can cause you to act before you think by activating fundamental motor functioning (movement) and emotional functioning (feelings) while short-circuiting the higher functions of the cerebral cortex, including thinking.[9]

Sometimes the amygdala's quick response is a good thing. For example, you're on safari in Africa, you see a lion running toward you, you're terrified, you instantly flee (fight or flight is the response that fear activates in the reptilian part of your brain). The amygdala just prevented you from becoming the lion's dinner. But, as Curran points out, in everyday life if you were to react solely from your amygdala, you would be operating mindlessly, responding with reflexive actions to everything you experience.[10] In other words, you would be on automatic pilot, allowing your machinery to run you 24/7!

When the amygdala causes you to react immediately to the threat of an approaching lion, it's doing its job, to evaluate threats.[11]

The problem is that the amygdala doesn't just identify an approaching lion as a threat; as you know from Part I, your default programming can interpret any event as a threat to your survival even when, in fact, it's not.

Using my earlier example, if your default programming interprets the comment "you don't understand" as someone telling you "you're wrong and stupid," and that, therefore, the person is rejecting you, the amygdala responds as if you are actually being threatened and in danger. On automatic pilot, you are interpreting that person's comment as a put-down and a threat to your survival when, in fact, it may not even be a put-down, let alone a threat. When you're on automatic pilot, a misinterpreted threat is as good as a real threat to stir the amygdala to react, causing you to respond defensively when there's no reason to be defensive.

When the amygdala responds based on the programming's misinterpretation of an event, your behavior will *always* be inappropriate because the amygdala isn't responding to the present event in a reality-based way; it's responding to your default programming's old interpretation of what it considers a similar past event. Curran observes that the factors that determine how and what your particular amygdala perceives as a threat are based on your life experiences up to that point.[12] This happens unconsciously.

Research on the brain has shown that the brain actually *embodies* this programming and that the amygdala uses it to assess threats to enable your survival. It's because the brain has embodied your programming—a process I'll describe in more detail later in this and the next several chapters—that the amygdala reacts so quickly and automatically. As I noted, it is calling the shots, often without your being conscious of the links being made between past and present events.

Until you begin to observe and reflect on your mind's thoughts and actions, you may have no idea that your amygdala is cueing actions based on a past experience, and that your brain embodies the belief that past behavior will protect your survival even if, in reality, that behavior is creating unnecessary problems. This is why the amygdala is often emotionally unintelligent.

The amygdala is keyed for your survival and functions self-centeredly. As Curran points out, selfishness, when it's appropriate, is good; you need some to survive, but you need to balance selfishness with selflessness.[13] How do you regulate the primitive, self-centered drives within your brain so that you can become an emotionally intelligent adult? How do you take control of your amygdala?[14] To put it another way: How do you transform yourself so that you are in charge instead of allowing your default programming to run you?

How Your Brain Develops Patterns of Behavior

Addressing this question from the perspective of research on the brain, the answer has to do with what Curran calls *templates*. A template is a pattern or model. In this context, the term signifies a pattern or model for behaviors, thus making it analogous to what I call programming. As Curran explains it, all social and other learning "is based on the development and maturation of templates."[15]

As children grow, their amygdala gathers information for survival behaviors, and they develop an enormous number of templates that allow them to do those survival behaviors with increasing efficiency.[16] Children learn, for example, to drink water from a glass and bring food on a fork to their mouths. It's the same with behavioral learning. For example, by being exposed repeatedly to behaviors that work socially, children develop the templates that they use to act appropriately in different social situations.[17] Because the amygdala is not large enough to store these templates, they are stored in the part of the cerebral cortex known as the *periorbital frontal cortex*, located behind and above your eyes.[18]

Around age eighteen months to two years, a toddler starts to develop a control system that can calm down and tame the amygdala's self-centered, reflexive, emotional character, which helps it to develop emotional control. By the time the child is eight years old, the control system is completely operational, and the child can apply these templates to modulate the amygdala's responses.[19]

Curran's explanation of the way these templates are formed in childhood is illuminating because it shows clearly how your interactions with your parents influence processes in your brain and how this affects your behavior. When your parents compliment you on what they consider good behavior, your brain releases a chemical called *dopamine*,[20] a *neurotransmitter* (chemical messenger) that shoots from one neuron to another across a juncture called a *synapse*.[21] The dopamine encourages the formation of the template that caused that particular behavior, and through this process, the "hardwiring" for the behavior becomes stronger.[22]

A more precise way to explain this is that the repeated "firing" of dopamine from one specific neuron to another specific neuron creates a *neural pathway* for the behavior. Neuropsychologist

Donald O. Hebb summed up the formation of the neural circuitry in our brain succinctly in what has become known as Hebb's Law: "Neurons that fire together wire together."[23] This is the physiological basis for how your programming and your machinery control your behavior when you're not acting mindfully: The neural pathways you develop from your experiences (and your interpretations of them) are your programming; the firing of neurons along these neural pathways that cause your behavior is your machinery.

Who we are reflects the relationship among our inherited DNA (biological), our experiences (environmental), and the formation of our brain and its influence on our behavior. The intention and commitment to change is vital to who you are and who you want to become. The way Curran explains this interrelationship and the potential you have to change your own "wiring" affirms the commitment I'm urging you to make to pursue self-transformation and expresses such transformation in terms of what research has taught us about the brain.

> You are the interaction between your genetic potentials and the myriad interactions those genetic potentials have with your environments. In your brain this lays down templates under the control of your emotional system. And those templates govern everything about how your brain, and therefore your self, functions. And it all comes down to wiring, the synaptic connections between your nerve cells. Which, of course, by appropriate work, can be remodeled to move you towards more complete emotional health.[24]

If you find that what Curran calls your wiring is cueing you to act in a way that doesn't serve you, *you can transform yourself to be more emotionally healthy by reprogramming yourself by remodeling—rewiring—your brain.* As neuroscientist Richard J. Davidson puts it in his book *The Emotional Life of Your Brain,* the emotional style from childhood that takes us into our lives as adults "doesn't need to be the one that describes us forever."[25]

The reason we have this potential is that the brain is malleable, and its malleability—what neuroscientists refer to as *neuroplasticity* or *brain plasticity*—gives us the ability to remodel it and to change our behavior.

To accomplish this remodeling, you need to be mindful: To interrupt your machinery, focus your mind on the present, observe your behavior, reflect on it, and make mindful choices about how you will act. If you notice certain areas in which your responses are inappropriate and dysfunctional and you're not in touch with your own and other people's feelings, it's a signal you need to develop new templates for personally and socially intelligent behavior that didn't develop sufficiently while you were growing up.

Let's say you have a tendency to take things for granted with little or no feeling or expression of gratitude. I'm not choosing this example arbitrarily. Gratitude is more than just good manners; scientists at the University of California at Davis conducted a study in which they found that people who wrote in a journal about five things they were grateful for each week developed a more positive outlook on the world, did more exercise, and didn't have as many physical problems as people in a similar group who didn't identify things they were grateful for. Other scientists have seen a link between gratefulness and lower blood pressure and a stronger immune system.[26]

If your parents or other role models didn't authentically express appreciation or encouragement, if you got the sense that saying "thank you" was a mere formality and didn't need to be connected to a real feeling of thanks, then you would need to start developing the template for gratitude. Building these templates requires a commitment to consciously recognize situations in which gratitude is an appropriate response. Making the conscious effort of opening yourself to experiencing this feeling when others are generous to you and communicating your gratitude to them as an expression of the feeling is how you build these new templates.

Initially, feeling grateful and expressing it might be like using a muscle you've never used before. But as you continue opening yourself to feeling and expressing gratitude, you'll develop a template for those behaviors, and it will become increasingly natural for you the more you do so. I've trained myself to thank people for sharing their feelings with me because I'm grateful for the trust they place in me through that sharing. The same principle applies if you lack a template for apologizing; the more you genuinely tell people you're sorry for something you've said or done that you regret, the more natural—and easier—it will become to do so.

Remodeling your brain for more emotionally healthy behavior also requires learning to identify the self-destructive behaviors that you unconsciously developed in response to past trauma. Without doing this, you are doomed to being run by the hardwiring that triggers behaviors that can hurt you and damage your relationships with others.

Your Unconscious Mind and the Wiring of Your Brain

It's important to remember that both your conscious and your unconscious mind influence the way your brain cues behavior. Indeed, your brain's hardwiring doesn't just come from your conscious mind. The unconscious mind, which holds the memories, traits, and feelings that your conscious mind finds too overwhelming to acknowledge or tolerate, can trigger your actions just as your conscious mind can.

Since behaviors that stem from your unconscious are hardwired in your brain, and since every time we repeat these behaviors we are reinforcing them, the things you hide from yourself have at least as much power over your behavior as the things that you are conscious of. I mentioned earlier that as a child I interpreted my parents' message about anger to mean that I should never be angry, that it was wrong, and I developed the belief that I needed to be super good so that nobody would be angry at me. That belief was so powerful that I hid my anger from myself, and only in my early thirties did I begin to be dimly aware of it through therapy. I now know that although I wasn't in touch with my anger emotionally, and didn't even acknowledge it intellectually, in fact I was filled with it, and at some level that anger was partially running me.

Although I didn't realize it as a child, I recognized later that I was angry at my older brother for not being there for me emotionally; enraged at my father for leaving me by dying; and angry at my mother because I felt that she was so fragile she couldn't be depended on if I needed emotional support; that, instead, I had to take care of her and myself, something that, as a child, I was completely unequipped to do. Later on, I was frustrated with all the people close to me whom I felt I needed to take care of when I also felt that they should do it for themselves. I believed it was up to me to take total responsibility for them and to give them everything they wanted, even though I didn't want to be an indentured servant.

It doesn't matter whether my interpretations of the experiences that led to this anger were entirely accurate; they were my perceptions, my interpretations, and the anger I felt was a result of what I subjectively experienced. I didn't recognize that my brother had his own machinery, which cut him off emotionally from me. I didn't allow myself to consider that I might be angry at my father for experiences I had with him during his lifetime, as it didn't seem fair to be angry at him because he died. I didn't recognize that my mother's delicate emotional state resulted from her own traumatic background.

I interpreted my mother's fragility as her strategy to communicate that I *had* to take care of her and of everything else if I wanted to survive. I *felt* that it was up to me to hold our whole world together. In hindsight it felt overwhelming, and it frightened me, and, as I mentioned, it made me angry that it was all up to me. I never expressed this anger to myself or to anyone. I just swallowed it down, hiding it while it grew and grew. The repetitive pattern of taking on the responsibility for others close to me reinforced the neural pathways for this behavior, thereby strengthening my caregiver programming, and that increased my anger.

With all this burning inside me, ready to explode, you'd think that I couldn't help but feel and recognize how angry I was, but I didn't. My defenses, on automatic, continued blocking my feelings of anger and rage as well as my ability to know that these feelings existed in me. But sometimes my anger, unbeknownst to me, would explode in situations with the people closest to me. If they confronted me by telling me how angry I was, I'd deny it. Gradually, in therapy, I came to understand that I had a lot of anger, and why I had hidden it from myself for so long.

In Jungian therapy, I learned about pioneer psychoanalyst Carl G. Jung's concept of the *dark side*, or the *shadow side*,[27] the place in our unconscious to which certain feelings and thoughts are banished because they don't go with our image of ourselves. For decades I kept my anger in my dark side. Jung said that as long as you keep parts of yourself in your shadow side, you deprive yourself of power. When you expose your shadow side to light and acknowledge the traits—the feelings, the aspects of your personality—you've been hiding, you turn the coal into a diamond.[28]

The shadow side is a psychological way to describe an aspect of the way our brain functions. As long as I allowed my default programming to continue to run me, with the belief that my anger was bad and dangerous instead of ever being justified and appropriate, the wiring of my brain kept me oblivious to my anger. I was also not conscious that my brain's wiring kept me acting in ways, including trying to suppress my anger, that made me even angrier. As I came to "own" my anger in therapy, I started to feel it, and I started to transform it from coal into a diamond. I began to integrate my anger as a legitimate part of me; when appropriate, I could express it, and claim the power to be more authentic with myself and with others.

Shining a light on the hidden anger in my shadow side allowed me to engage in the process of creating new neural pathways instead of allowing the old neural pathways to estrange me from my angry feelings. Creating new neural pathways is a process I liken to blazing a path through a field of high grass through which no one has walked before. It takes a lot of effort to walk through the high grass the first time, but if you repeatedly walk through the field following the same trajectory, gradually you flatten the grass on that trajectory and create a path that eventually becomes easier and more comfortable to walk on. It takes commitment to remodel your brain by creating new neural pathways, but in time it will make your life easier!

PAUSE YOUR MACHINERY

- Think mindfully about whether you're hiding any aspects of yourself in your shadow side because your conscious mind finds them unacceptable to your image of yourself. Have you believed, for example, that anger is "wrong" or "bad" and that you're a good person and, therefore, you are never angry? If not, are there other thoughts and feelings that, when you think about it mindfully, you suspect you've been keeping in your shadow side? If so, write them down.

- In addition, write down what you think it costs you to keep these thoughts and feelings in your shadow side. For example, if you feel that you've kept your anger in your shadow side, look back on the last two weeks and think mindfully about whether there are times when it would have been appropriate for you to be in touch with your anger about how another person acted toward you. What did it cost you to deny your feelings and withhold your emotions?

Continuing with this example, also think about whether there are times when you have acted angrily without acknowledging it or taking responsibility for it; maybe you realize that your machinery was keeping it hidden. How did hiding it from yourself affect your relationship with others?

- Think mindfully about ways you act in certain situations that you now recognize as dysfunctional because they result in you not getting what you want, resulting in you feeling frustrated and unfulfilled. Make a list of these dysfunctional habits, and be sure to keep it! It's a preliminary list of behaviors you want to change by creating new neural pathways that will lead you to act in healthier, more productive ways.

Over the next several chapters, we'll look in more detail at the relationship between your mind and your brain and at how you can use your mind to remodel your brain.

CHAPTER SIX

USING YOUR MIND TO CHANGE YOUR BRAIN AND YOUR BEHAVIOR

..... 🧠 .....

"We are always in a perpetual state of being created and creating ourselves," says Daniel J. Siegel, M.D., co-director of UCLA's Mindful Awareness Research Center and author,[1] whose work I read and then experienced on a more personal level through a course in mindful awareness at UCLA. His research and observations provide valuable insights that both substantiate the fact that we can use our mind to remodel our brain and clarify why and how we can do so.

You might recall that, in Chapter 1, I mentioned the saying "The mind is what the brain does for a living." Siegel emphasizes the reciprocal effect of the mind on the brain and the brain on the mind. While some scientists credit the brain with creating the mind or see the mind as "the activity of the brain," he explains that actually "the mind uses the brain to create itself" and that "the mind and the brain reinforce each other."[2] This means that the way you use your mind utilizes your brain in specific ways that contribute to the individual nature of your mind and your brain.

Siegel's definition of the mind underscores why the *way* you use it is so vital. The mind, he says, is an "embodied [meaning it's in your physical body] relational [meaning it's involved both in what's happening within you and in your relationships with others] process of regulating the flow of energy and information."[3]

Energy gives you the ability to do; information tells you what to do. The ways your mind directs the energy and information flow throughout your neural network molds your neural pathways, creating your brain's hardwiring,[4] the physical embodiment in your brain of what I call your programming. So you can say that when you're on automatic pilot your machinery's programming, or your hardwiring, produces your behavior.

As you know, the process of creating your programming starts early in life. Research on the brain has revealed that childhood experiences have an effect on how the brain functions and on its structure.[5] Research also explains why and how mindful awareness is effective in remodeling your brain and achieving the kind of structural changes that are necessary for transformation.

"The way you use your mind will transform your brain,"[6] says Siegel, because the way you use your mind drives the flow of energy and information in a particular manner, and "the brain embeds the pathways of energy and information flow."[7] So the way in which you pay attention changes your brain's physiology by driving the energy and information along certain neural circuits and not along others.[8] With mindful awareness, you drive energy and information along new neural pathways that create healthier behavior than the neural pathways that your early experiences created and that have become your default programming.

I've discussed mindful awareness as being fully in the present with an open rather than a judgmental attitude, which gives us the ability to make conscious, productive choices instead of allowing ourselves to act and react on automatic pilot. Paraphrasing molecular biologist Jon Kabat-Zinn, an important researcher in the field of mindful awareness, Siegel defines that term as "paying attention in the present moment without holding onto judgments and doing this with intention [purpose]."[9]

We might think that simply being aware would be enough, but as we've discussed and Siegel affirms, ordinary awareness is filled with interpretations and judgments.[10] For example, suppose you use a steak knife to cut a piece of cake to snack on and you accidentally cut your finger. Exercising ordinary awareness, you might judge yourself critically. You might tell yourself you're stupid or a klutz, especially because you used a *steak* knife. You might think the cut was "payback" for eating cake in the first place since it's loaded with empty calories. Ordinary awareness generally contains all sorts of variations on the four negative beliefs about yourself: *something is wrong; I'm not good enough; I don't belong here;* and *I'm always going to be on my own.*

Critical judgments like these, which are part of ordinary awareness, create suffering. But suffering from your own self-judgments is unneeded,[11] and it's dysfunctional. Why beat yourself up because you accidentally hurt yourself? You add the pain of feeling bad about yourself to the physical pain of cutting your finger. And the anxiety you add through self-criticism can take your mind off what you really need to do, which is to apply first aid to your finger to stop the bleeding.

Again, being mindfully aware means being aware without judgment; it is being aware of what is, and accepting it as just what it is. With mindful awareness, you see your finger being cut as just a fact, without any judgments or interpretations, and then you focus on what needs to be done to take care of your finger. Mindful awareness doesn't mean that judgmental thoughts won't pass through your mind; it means that you won't seize and hold onto them. Instead, you just let them pass as if they are clouds in the sky.

A Closer Look at Mindful Awareness and Why Developing It Is a Gift to Yourself

Mindful awareness is more than just an absence of judgments; mindful awareness adds positive qualities to awareness. Mindful awareness, as Siegel further defines it, is *paying attention in the moment with curiosity, openness, acceptance, and love of and compassion for yourself.* He uses the acronym COAL to describe this state and to make it easier to remind ourselves of the qualities that characterize it.

C stands for curiosity (inquiring without being judgmental).

O stands for openness (having the freedom to experience what is occurring as simply the truth, without judgments).

A stands for acceptance (taking as a given the reality of and the need to be precisely where you are).

L stands for love (being kind, compassionate, and empathetic to others and to yourself).[12]

Love of and compassion for yourself are the opposite of being unempathetic, self-punishing, and filled with self-criticisms and judgments. If you've had parents who were very critical, the inner critic in you may have a loud and persistent voice, and it may be difficult to be loving and compassionate to yourself because it's unfamiliar. With mindful awareness, even though critical thoughts may pass through your head, you can remind yourself that the judgments are just coming from your default programming, and you can start to parent yourself by developing love and compassion for yourself. Mindful awareness will keep you from holding on to judgments and looking at them as if they were "the truth." Remember that the voice in your head isn't you; it's just part of you, and it's often wrong!

I like to use the common habit of procrastination as an example of the benefit of being mindfully aware instead of self-judging. If you're a procrastinator, when you find yourself faced with something that will take you out of your comfort zone or that you're required to do but for some other reason don't want to do, you'll put it off and put it off until the eleventh hour—or later—at which point you say to yourself, "Now I *really* have to do it."

If you're self-critical and beat yourself up for procrastinating, your machinery fills up with negative thoughts and your body fills up with negative feelings, which will distract you from the task at hand. You might even build up the task in your mind as "impossible," and you may even give up on doing it, which will only give you another reason to judge yourself and beat yourself up. By contrast, with mindful awareness you will be in the present and you will see only the facts of the situation. Judgments will simply pass through your mind, without your attaching weight to them, and letting go of the self-judgments will make it easier for you to focus your energy and attention on completing the task. In practicing such mindful awareness, you will demonstrate the qualities that Siegel calls COAL, especially having love and compassion for yourself.

Whether it's procrastination or some other habitual behavior that you feel doesn't serve you, once you've identified your pattern it's easier to make mindful choices that will help you stop automatically following your old default programming and commit to creating new neural pathways for more effective behavior.

Siegel points out that once mindful awareness awakens within you, a natural progression takes place and you become reflective about your own mental processes and patterns, and this is what enables you to make new, healthier choices and to change.[13] With mindfulness, you become more attuned to yourself,[14] and you become more attuned to others. "Our minds connect with one another via neural circuitry in our bodies that is hard-wired to take in others' signals,"[15] he explains. The more attuned we are to other people, the better our relationships will be.

Yet, despite knowing the many benefits of mindfulness, some of us habitually let our hardwiring—our machinery's default programming—run us on automatic pilot instead of practicing mindful awareness. This causes us to be stuck in old patterns that constantly prevent us from getting what we truly want: connection and attunement with ourselves, with others, and with the Universe. This is why it's crucial for us to choose to live more and more in the COAL state of mindfulness that allows us to be present in our own lives and to make choices that create more aliveness and joy. In other words, *to be in the moment, in the now.*

One of the biggest benefits of the mindful state is that it alleviates the conflict that occurs in our inner world when what life presents to us is different from our picture of how we think it "should be." When our inner world is fixed on our expectations and they go unfulfilled, and we're on automatic pilot, we experience disappointment, frustration, and anger over the fact that what's happening isn't what we've anticipated.

In this condition, we become unable to act effectively in the circumstances in which we find ourselves. We may be so upset that we just don't act at all, or we react based on our disappointment, stress, or any of the other emotions that our machinery triggers in us, and, if we do so, we make the situation worse by not acting in a more appropriate way that would help us achieve the best outcome in that situation.

We are designed to react to everything; the only choice we have is about *how* we react!

The following three situations always result in upsets:

1. Unfulfilled expectations
2. Thwarted intentions
3. Incomplete communication (By this I mean a situation in which you've expressed something that you realize wasn't really received by the other person or in which you wanted to express something that you never actually expressed.)

Each of these three situations conflicts with our "pictures/shoulds," which is why, if we're on automatic pilot, we become upset. This is when the COAL state of mindfulness is so beneficial: When you are curious, open, accepting, and loving, you will let your judgments about how the situation "should be" pass through your mind, but you won't attach any weight to them. You'll know that this interpretation is coming from your hardwiring, your programming. When you are in the curious, open, accepting, loving state of mindfulness, you'll be in the moment. Instead of listening to the voice in your head, with its negativity, its judgments of the situation, and its self-judgments—which would result in your shutting down and/or acting inappropriately—you'll be able to make mindful choices about how to respond.

When we set our mind on a certain objective and life delivers us an outcome other than the one we intended or hoped for, and that our mind judges to be an inferior one, we experience an unfulfilled expectation or a thwarted intention. If we react on automatic pilot, we'll experience disappointment, frustration, and, possibly, anger. Often, when reacting automatically to situations in which we're facing an unfulfilled expectation or a thwarted intention, we also spend a great deal of time bemoaning what has happened and lose ourselves in sorrow or self-pity or in blaming others or ourselves.

If we respond to the situation automatically, our ability to make productive choices will be sabotaged by these machinery-generated emotions and by all the past experiences that, consciously or unconsciously, our programming is bringing into the present circumstance. If, instead, we respond to the situation mindfully, with curiosity, openness, acceptance, and love, we can look at and experience the situation as simply what it is, a fact—just "what is"—and make a *choice* about how to respond to "what is" that will be healthier and more responsible to ourselves and to whomever else may be part of the situation.

The same applies to a situation that involves incomplete communication, that is, things that were important for you to express to other people that those other people didn't hear or that you may not have expressed. This creates the same kinds of stressful feelings that, when you're on automatic pilot, cause you to ruminate instead of acting responsibly. When you're mindful about undelivered communications, when you view the situation with curiosity, openness, acceptance, and love, you recognize that you're upset because the communication wasn't received in the way you wanted it to be, or that you never actually expressed it, and you can make a mindful choice about what you want to communicate and the best way to communicate it.

In other words, when you're mindful, you are actually *experiencing the present* and are able to respond the way you *choose* to respond in the moment, rather than the way you have been *wired* to respond automatically, full of judgments and interpretations but without any true thought. By making mindful choices, you are productively using Hebb's Law—neurons that fire together wire together—and also starting to rewire your brain, which is the road to self-transformation.

PAUSE YOUR MACHINERY

- Think about whether you've had an upset in the last few days. You may have had more than one, but just choose one of them, preferably the one that has the most power over you, perhaps even days after the event. Write down whether the upset was the result of an unfulfilled expectation, a thwarted intention, or an incomplete communication.

- Write a description of how you reacted to the upset. What did you say? How did you act? If you reacted to another person, describe how your words and behavior seemed to affect him or her.

- Reflect on your reaction. Write down whether it was a mindful or an automatic response caused by your programming. If you reacted on automatic pilot, describe how you could react mindfully if you have the same upset in the future. (Because you undoubtedly will!)

In the next chapter, we'll look at some of the major ways that your dysfunctional programming affects your behavior and how you can use mindful awareness to disconnect from your programming and make new and healthier choices about how to act.

CHAPTER SEVEN

MINDFUL AWARENESS: THE KEY TO DISENGAGING FROM YOUR DYSFUNCTIONAL PROGRAMMING

The first step toward enlightenment is recognizing that the voice in your head isn't you, that it's not your boss, and that it may or may not be accurate. When you are mindfully aware, you recognize this. Mindfulness lets you disengage from the critical and often dictatorial voice that repeats your "shoulds" and engage in the present with "what is."

Daniel Siegel, M.D., uses the word *discernment* to describe the outgrowth of mindfulness that makes it possible to separate yourself from the voice in your head. He defines discernment as a "process . . . in which it becomes possible to be aware that your mind's activities are not the totality of who you are."[1] By giving you the ability to separate yourself from the voice in your head, discernment allows you to view it from a new perspective that helps you move beyond its limitations.

I like Siegel's description of this process of discerning what is going on in your mind rather than just automatically believing it without questioning it:

> Discernment is a form of dis-identification from the activity of your own mind: As you SIFT through your mind (being aware of sensations, images, feelings and thoughts) you come to see these activities of the mind as just waves at the surface of the mental sea . . . This capacity to disentangle oneself from the chatter of the mind, to discern that these are "just activities of the mind," is liberating and, for many, revolutionary. At its essence, this discernment is how mindfulness may help alleviate suffering.
>
> Discernment also gives us the wisdom of how to interact with each other with more thoughtfulness and compassion . . . By getting beneath our automatic mental habits, we are freed to engage with each other with a deeper sense of connection and empathy.[2]

This hits home for me because it summarizes what I've observed in myself as I've worked to become more mindful. "Dis-identification from the activity of your own mind" is a precise and powerful way to describe knowing that the voice in your head isn't you.

Looking back, I now see that before I began therapy, the "eggshell" I was living in was devoid of enlightenment because I was still totally "in my mind," believing that the voice in my head was me and vice versa. I didn't understand that my mind's "chatter" was "just activities of the mind" or "just waves at the surface of the mental sea"; I believed that my mind was always telling me the truth and that I had to listen to it as if it was the law of the land.

My first awakening that there was more to me than the voice in my head came when the therapist prompted me to examine my childhood. His questions, asking me to look beyond the "normal" and "regular" labels I'd always put on my childhood, helped me begin to recognize that losing my father was traumatic and that my absence of childhood memories only confirmed the enormity of the trauma of my father's death. Therapy set me on the road to being mindful, to learning that the voice in my head isn't me, and to begin disengaging from my dysfunctional mental habits based on my past programming.

The information I've shared with you about the brain clarifies why what you learn about yourself through mindfulness can create tangible results. But I don't want just to give you this information. I want to provide you with a road map for becoming mindfully aware of how you operate. Within the road map I'll offer you specific ways you can use mindfulness to recognize patterns that produce self-sabotaging behavior, which becomes habitual, and I'll share with you how to use mindfulness to make new, healthier choices, remodel your brain, and transform your life.

A Road Map for Becoming Mindfully Aware of How You Operate

One of the concepts I find valuable in helping me to mindfully look at how I think and act when I allow my default programming to run me is the concept of *identity*. By identity I mean the way that we present ourselves to the world when we're on automatic pilot.

Our identity can include an infinite combination of personality attributes, qualities, and patterns of behavior that become part of our image, and our identity is complex because different aspects of it may come into play in different situations. We want to be a different character to someone we want to date than we are to someone from whom we want to borrow money. Some aspects of our identity may even lie dormant for years. All of it is our identity, however, and we show its different facets to the outside world depending on how life unfolds and how, when we're on automatic pilot, our machinery responds to the different circumstances in which we find ourselves.

Step 1: Recognize Your Identity and How It Keeps You Trapped

Your identity, with all its aspects, is a way that you've invented and refined, often without being consciously aware of it, to cope with past situations, starting in childhood. It's part of your programming and embodied in your hardwiring. And that's the problem: Once your identity is formed, your machinery keeps you stuck, repetitively playing the same roles that are part of your identity. This makes it hard to break out of the patterns of behavior, attitudes, and points of view that are aspects of your identity and that, because you are not conscious that your identity is programmed, you believe are the true you.

As long as you're on automatic pilot, you're in your identity, and *your identity is a fixed way of being, albeit with many costumes into which you can change to present yourself as a variety of sub-characters.* The vital word in this definition is *fixed*: Even though your identity has different aspects, different roles—many of which contradict each other—that you play in different situations, your identity and all the roles it consists of are static, unchanging.

Regardless of how many roles your identity is made up of, regardless of how much energy you put into your identity and how vital other people may perceive it to be, *operating on automatic pilot within the confines of your identity robs you of aliveness and makes spontaneity impossible.* Operating within the confines of your identity is like imprisoning yourself; you have little or no room in which to move or air to breathe. To free yourself, you have to become aware of what your identity is, learn to dis-identify with it, and make mindful choices in the present.

Step 2: Recognize the Acts That Make Up Your Identity

The primary components that make up your identity are your *acts*, that is, the character roles you play in your interactions with others. Metaphorically speaking, you're in movie after movie, all with different stories and problems, but you may always wind up playing the same character type. Maybe you're the town drunk or the "go-to-guy" or the hooker with the heart of gold. Your acts may be Clint Eastwood–like (righteous, direct, to the point) or they may have a shape-shifter quality, making you like a chameleon within your identity, varying your acts widely with the situation. These roles are programmed strategies, which you've been developing since childhood, to cope with various situations, especially those that your mind perceives as problems.

But, as with all aspects of your identity, your acts are fixed. So, even though different acts may come into play in different circumstances, *when you're doing any of your acts, you're not in the present; you're doing a routine that keeps you in the past,* which means you're not open to experiencing what is actually happening here and now.

You can start the process of dis-identifying with and disengaging from your identity by learning to recognize (or to use Siegel's terminology, discern) your acts.

You may have thought that the childhood experiences that exert a powerful influence on you are just those associated with the memories you think about. But brain research tells us that *whether you remember your childhood experiences or not, they influence the physiology of your brain.* As Siegel explains, "Early experiences shape the structure and function of the brain."[3] This is *how* your identity and all its acts become hardwired, and it's *why* you need to be mindful to learn to recognize them and disengage from them. When you do this, instead of acting in the world within the confines of your identity, you will be in the moment, which means that you will be free to just "*be.*"

MY "POOR ME" ACT

When I learned the concept of acts, I set myself the task of mindfully observing my thoughts and behavior to learn what my acts were.

I began to see, for example, that in situations in which I felt shamed and blamed, the chatter in my mind was something like, "How could that person start shaming me like this, doesn't he know how much I've already suffered since I was eleven!" or "How could that person start blaming me, doesn't she know I'm wounded and damaged because my father died when I was little!" I began to notice, too, that in these situations, physically and vocally, I would act the part of the vulnerable "poor me" little boy as a way of stopping what I perceived as an attack and, instead, eliciting sympathy.

Let me stop for a moment here to explain that all of our acts—and our identity as a whole, really—have three payoffs:

1. We get to be right and make others wrong.
2. We get to dominate others or, at the very least, avoid having them dominate us.
3. We get to justify ourselves and, in the process, often invalidate others.

Looked at from this perspective, my "poor me" act was my programmed strategy for making myself right because my machinery perceived the other person as trying to make me wrong. "Of course I'm right!" my act declares, but not by saying that the behavior for which I was being criticized was "right." Rather, I was right because I was emotionally stunted as a result of my father's death; it was the only behavior I was capable of, so others needed to give me space! Anyone who asked more of me was *wrong* to expect, and certainly wrong to demand, anything else!

My poor-me act also was aimed at fending off what my machinery perceived as another person's trying to dominate me by shaming and blaming me into a subordinate position. Since my poor-me act includes the position that I "need . . . help" and that the other person is "bad" if he or she doesn't "help me," this act of mine is also a strategy to dominate the other person by making him or her help me, that is, come to my aid in whatever I want.

Thus my poor-me act justified me (and my behavior) and invalidated the other person by declaring that he or she was wrong to demand, expect, or even request anything of me other than what, in my "poor me" state, I was capable of.

As you start to look for the acts that are part of your identity, keep in mind that they may not be consistent with each other. For example, my poor-me act, which portrays me as damaged and powerless, is inconsistent with another of my acts, which I've labeled "the designated hitter" because it portrays me as the hero who's ready to take over. My machinery uses these acts in different situations—or even at different times in the same situation.

PAYOFFS OR HEAVY COSTS?

I've mentioned that our acts have three payoffs, but are these really payoffs?

By becoming mindfully aware of and reflecting on my acts, I can now see that they don't deliver real payoffs; they're just payoffs for my machinery. They keep me trapped in my old fixed way of being and reinforce the neural pathways that keep me in the loop of repeating the same behaviors again and again. They make it impossible to connect authentically with other people and to experience true connection, which is pure love.

Our identity is part of the defense system we form as an unconscious strategy for survival, to cope with the fear of being wrong, being controlled, being invalidated, or being abandoned. Your identity and its various roles are elements of your defense system, and they cut you off from your real feelings. They cost you self-expression, satisfaction, vitality, and well-being.

My poor-me act may get the person I feel is shaming or blaming me to feel sorry for me and stop what I hear as criticism, but it keeps me stuck as a victim, a wounded child, instead of allowing me to be a fully functioning adult. While it attempts to manipulate others for sympathy, it stops me from relating with integrity and robs me of my own power, strength, and potential. It also blocks information that could be helpful to me in my desire to grow. So while this act of mine is intended to excuse me from what I perceive as shame and blame, it's at the cost of closing myself off from a productive conversation that might lead to my learning about areas in which I would benefit by changing.

Step 3: Recognize the Clues That Help You Disengage from Your Acts

It's challenging to recognize and dis-identify with the mental chatter associated with our acts. We're so used to the voice in our head talking to us in certain ways—the ways that it is wired to—that we may succumb to the programmed message that the voice is telling us as if it's the truth. But if we stay mindful, we'll be in the moment, and instead of believing what our mind is saying, we'll hear it simply as chatter, the content of which can give us clues to the distinctive nature and purpose of our acts, and to the particular behavior that the voice is attempting to cue us to go into.

Generally, we go into our acts so mindlessly that we're not even aware of the accompanying chatter that cues it; we're so used to that particular kind of talk going on in our head that we accept it without question. A situation occurs and we automatically go into our act. When you're mindful, however, you can start hearing this chatter and recognizing it as a clue that informs you that you're about to go into your act or that you're already in it.

As with the chatter, your feelings are another major clue. You may discover that you have very specific feelings associated with an act. These are always past-based feelings (and thus are not authentic feelings), and they are triggered by your programming, most often in response to a perceived danger. You need to be in the present to experience authentic feelings.

For example, the feelings associated with my poor-me act come in like an invisible cloud of anxiety that stems from self-doubt; they are the handiwork of my machinery's favorite tools, the self-critic (who is sometimes a terrorist in the degree of self-criticism he spews). I start feeling bad about myself, isolated, and I want to close down. I feel desperate to throw off these feelings that come from my perception that I'm being shamed and blamed. I became aware of this through mindfully looking at what I was feeling as my mind's chatter started to cue the act. You might notice that the same old feelings and images you had as a child are associated with some of your acts too.

I want to emphasize that recognizing, dis-identifying with, and disengaging from the acts that make up your identity is a process; it doesn't happen all at once. Some of my acts have taken me years to put behind me. Recognizing your acts is the first step, but recognizing them doesn't mean that suddenly you'll stop doing them. Once you're mindfully aware of an act, you can interrupt your machinery from triggering that particular behavior and start to build a new neural pathway for a different behavior. Again, you've been doing your acts for years—they're hardwired—so you can't expect them to disappear overnight. The vital thing is to be mindful and to stay committed to the process of recognizing and disengaging from your acts.

It's important to realize that, after you start this process, it's almost impossible to stop your machinery from going on automatic pilot when you encounter a problematic situation that triggers your acts. When this happens, you have a true opportunity afterward to review the situation mindfully, which will start building the neural pathways for a more constructive behavior for next time. Remember that mindfulness isn't just being aware; as Siegel's acronym reminds us, it's a COAL state of mind: being curious, open, accepting, and loving. If you start judging yourself for having gone into your act, focus on being mindful and let the judgments pass through your mind without holding on to them. When you do this, rather than being judgmental, you will be curious about how you acted, open about the situation and yourself, and accepting of and loving to yourself.

The process of recognizing, dis-identifying with, and disengaging from your acts needs to be a loving and supportive one. It's part of parenting yourself. Remember, giving free rein to your self-critic is part of your past programming and only serves to keep you in the past, your personal prison, instead of moving you toward your goal to transform yourself, which can only take place in the present.

Today's Temporary Changes Become Tomorrow's New Traits

The more you recognize, dis-identify with, and disengage from your acts, the less frequently you will go into them. I found this to be true without realizing the neurological process that supports it.

Research on the brain has demonstrated that *all of the changes we make through mindful awareness, which at first are temporary, lead to new traits, new ways of behaving, by changing the brain.* Mindlessly doing the same things, such as automatically going into your acts, reinforces your existing neural firing patterns, which keeps your behavior the same as it's always been. As Siegel explains, mindful awareness ("using your intention to pay attention") "gives rise to changes in the way [you] live." Indeed, through mindful awareness, you "sculpt" your brain toward mental health.[4]

Again, the reason this is possible is because our brain is malleable, or neuroplastic. The good news, then, is that as sculptors of our own brain, we are not working with a hard substance like marble. When a sculptor cuts away the stone, that piece of marble is gone. From that point on, the sculptor is stuck with the marble statue as it is, regardless of whether the sculptor likes the way it looks after he or she has chiseled it.

But the brain is not marble; it is malleable, like clay. The neural pathways of our wiring are not carved in stone; they are in our neuroplastic brain, which means that if we don't like the way a neural pathway was formed at a particular fork in the road of our life, we don't have to live with that particular cut from that point on. When our old hardwiring triggers our fixed identity and its acts, and we realize that they are working against us rather than for us, we can create new neural pathways that will allow us to be in the present and to act authentically and appropriately. The only tool we need is mindful awareness.

Siegel describes five qualities associated with mindful awareness, and I see these as the antithesis of, and the antidote to, our fixed identity and its acts. The acronym he provides for these qualities is FACES:

F = flexible

A = adaptive

C = coherent

E = energized

S = stable[5]

And Siegel uses these terms in very specific ways: Being flexible means that you can take in information about a situation in the present, give yourself time to reflect, and make a choice about how to respond appropriately. Being adaptive (which flexibility opens the door to and enhances) means having the capacity to cope in a healthy way with new situations as well as changes in old situations. Being coherent means feeling connected to yourself and other people, open, harmonious, and engaged with and receptive to life. It gives you a sense that life is always new and of inner knowing, compassion and empathy. ("Coherence," Siegel says, "in many ways describes well-being."[6]) Being energized means that the energy that gives you the capacity to authentically engage in life is abundantly available and moves without blockages. Being stable means that, although you may react at times in a way that's more automatic than mindful, you return to a state of emotional equilibrium.[7]

Focusing on these beneficial qualities—the ability to be flexible, adaptive, coherent, energized, and stable—reminds you why you're working to recognize, dis-identify with, and disengage from your acts. Your acts prevent you from incorporating these qualities in your responses to the world. Indeed, your acts make you the polar opposite: inflexible, nonadaptive, incoherent, unenergized, and unstable. When you are in an act, you are not connected to yourself or to others, and you are unreceptive. Your acts block energy. A shorthand way of saying all of this is that your acts are your machinery's personas that keep you stuck.

The crucial point to remember is that, as with the voice in your head, *the acts are not you; they are just a construct of your machinery's programming in response to fears that arose in earlier situations.* They keep you in the past and cost you aliveness and joy. They keep you out of touch with your being, with your true feelings, with your sense of connectedness to yourself, to others, to Higher Power. When you are into your acts you are really not present; you're just in your machinery, being run by your programming.

By using mindful awareness to recognize your behavior and to dis-identify with and disengage from your acts, you are creating new neural pathways with the ultimate effect of remodeling your brain and transforming yourself and your experience of life!

PAUSE YOUR MACHINERY

- Think mindfully about your "acts"—the character roles you play in your interactions with others when you react on automatic pilot, especially in times of stress. Write a brief description of each act.
- It's helpful to label each of your acts with a short phrase that gives you a quick handle on it. You might also include a satirical

element in your labels for your acts to help distance you from them. For example, if one of your acts is to save people close to you whom you perceive as being in trouble, you might label your act "The Superhero" or "The Superheroine." Or if one of your acts is to stay on the sidelines and feel sorry for yourself for doing so, you might label it "The Pitiful Wallflower."

- After labeling your act, describe it more fully, including the attitudes and traits that are part of it. For example, if your identity is that of a caregiver, and one of your acts is "The Good Doctor" or "The Good Nurse" or "The Human Band-Aid," does your act include the attitude that you always have to take care of other people's needs and feelings, even at the expense of your own? If so, does this mean that you believe you should always agree to other people's requests even if you would really like not to?

- Write down the false payoffs that you get from each act. Then write down what each of your acts costs you. Imagine life without the need to cover your true Self with an act.

Now that we've looked at your acts and how you can recognize, dis-identify with, and disengage from them, let's take a look at how you can distinguish and disengage from the destructive beliefs you may not even know you have that affect your behavior when you're on automatic pilot.

CHAPTER EIGHT

LEARNING TO RECOGNIZE AND LET GO OF SELF-DEFEATING BELIEFS

····· 🧠 ·····

In addition to your acts, your identity also includes your beliefs about yourself and the world, which underlie your behavior. I call these beliefs your *Organizing Principles*. Organizing Principles are developed early on and become embedded in your default programming. These beliefs express the way you view the world and your individual place in it. Your machinery interprets these beliefs as facts (not as past-based feelings, which they actually are) and uses them as filters as it scans everything around you—and that's the problem! Your Organizing Principles (like the other aspects of your identity) keep you trapped in the past where they originated, and they frequently prevent you from hearing and seeing what is actually happening in the present.

When you are on automatic pilot, instead of clearly seeing what's right in front of you, your Organizing Principles—that is, your attitudes and points of view—because they act as filters, limit you to perceiving the world through the interpretations in your default programming and trigger you to respond based on those perceptions.

Whenever we have a new experience, within a nanosecond our machinery conducts a file search and comes up with a situation it interprets to be a similar situation from the past. Our machinery then gives us a "Go!" based on that interpretation, and we react based on the Organizing Principle our mind decides is applicable.

Thus, based on your Organizing Principles, your mind responds to new experiences by automatically searching your old database of responses to past situations and reacting—without your being aware of it—by using your pre-programmed expectations. Often these expectations are based on misinterpretations of what you are hearing and seeing and on your programming's expectations of what is okay and what is not okay.

In other words, the beliefs that I refer to as your Organizing Principles are so embedded that when you're on automatic pilot, they *create* the way you perceive whatever is happening, even though you think that you're perceiving it objectively.

The reason your Organizing Principles can keep you from hearing and seeing what other people are really expressing is that the mind is an extremely elegant operating system with the ability to instantly process incoming data as it arrives. The pitfall of this processing is that the mind jumps to conclusions.

As soon as the mind hears or sees "just enough" to fit its expectations—which are generally guided by its programming—it draws conclusions about the other person's communication, even if the conclusions would be proven wrong by fully listening to the complete message. The net result is that because we so often hear and see based on past expectations, we distort new input based on what we're expecting, even if these expectations are inaccurate. We believe we really listened or saw when we only got part of the story.

Mark Twain commented on the power of the mind to distort what we perceive this way: "You can't depend on your eyes when your imagination is out of focus." What makes what Twain calls your "imagination" out of focus? Your programming, including your underlying beliefs and expectations about the world and about yourself.

When you allow your machinery to run you, your interpretations of past experiences will cue you to hear only what your machinery expects you to hear and see what it expects you to see regardless of the treasures that the present may be offering you. They will also cue you to react according to your default programming even if you think you're choosing to react the way you do because it's "the right way" to react to what you are hearing and seeing.

Here's a visual image that illustrates how your perspective determines your perceptions. It also illustrates that the instructions you receive—which, when you're on automatic pilot, come from your programming—determine your perspective.

Look at the following drawing (designed by early-twentieth-century Danish psychologist Edgar Rubin), which can be perceived as a white candlestick against a black background.

Now look at it again and flip your perspective so you see it as a silhouette of two faces in profile, their noses, lips, and foreheads almost touching. When you view it this way, the white candlestick is now the white background behind the two faces. All it takes to totally transform how you see the drawing is using mindfulness to switch your focus and see the picture in a different way.

When we're on automatic pilot, it doesn't occur to us that what we're seeing (and hearing) is an interpretation based on our machinery's perceptions. We don't realize that we can flip our perspective by letting go of the Organizing Principles that are filtering and determining our initial perspective. But if we do so, we will perceive in a different and—in the case of letting go of our Organizing Principles—a more accurate way.

The most insidious thing is that the more unconscious you are of the beliefs that make up your Organizing Principles, the more power they have over you. The more entrenched you are in believing that they are facts and not beliefs, the less likely you are to question them. When you don't recognize that your beliefs are instructing you about how to hear and see the world, you get locked into seeing the drawing as a candlestick; the thought doesn't enter your mind that you could flip your perspective, look at the drawing differently, and see it as profiles of two faces.

Uncover Your Organizing Principles

Take this opportunity to uncover your Organizing Principles, see their limitations, and flip your perspective—all of which will start the process of no longer letting them run you.

My Organizing Principles have been:

1. The world isn't safe; don't trust.

2. Painful feelings are dangerous. (The corollary is all feelings have the potential to be painful, so all feelings are dangerous.)

3. I must stay in control to be safe.

4. No one will take care of my needs but me.

5. Hang in there. I can make things happen.

6. Avoid rejection and abandonment: Don't risk losing the love attachment bond.

7. Relationships between parents and children take precedence over all other relationships.

8. I'm not qualified to handle painful situations. That takes a real adult, and in my inner world I'm still a vulnerable kid.

9. If they (anyone close to me) loved me, they would never put me in this terrible position (meaning the position of asking me to do something I don't want to do).

10. Eventually, loving others will make things work out.

11. I'm a good guy and I never hurt anyone unjustly.

I learned that the first step in uncovering your Organizing Principles is to recognize that you have them; that very specific beliefs, many of which you may never have consciously articulated to yourself, underlie and cause you to see, hear, and act as you do. Once you recognize this, you can start to look mindfully to see what these beliefs are. Here are my suggestions for how you can do this.

Define Your Beliefs

One way is to see if you can define your beliefs (and the behavior that results from them) by contrasting them with the beliefs of other people around you whose attitudes and actions strike you as very different from your own. Analyzing these differences can help you recognize and put into words what your underlying beliefs are.

I came to realize I had the Organizing Principle "The world isn't safe; don't trust" when I noticed how different a close friend's overall attitude about the world was from mine. I saw that she generally expected things to go well and for people to do what she wanted and expected them to do. This struck me as odd because it was the opposite of how I felt; I approached situations ready to protect myself, believing that old axiom, "Whatever can go wrong will go wrong if I give it the space to." I started wondering what caused the difference between my friend's perspective and mine, and I realized I believed that "the world isn't safe; don't trust."

When I realized I didn't trust the world the way my friend did, I started becoming mindful about my thoughts—the chatter in my mind—about not trusting. I started noticing my default position that in certain types of situations the suspicions and fears expressed by the voice in my head were keeping me from being in the now. I came to see that the anxiety that accompanied these daily situations resulted from my default programming's belief system of mistrust.

Fear of abandonment is a core issue in my programming, creating anxiety in me based on strong feelings from the past, related to having been abandoned (my father's death, my mother's unavailability). This core issue gave rise to a default belief in my programming that I cannot depend on people to be there for me. "The world isn't safe, don't trust" voices my programming's fear that I can't trust relationships with other people because ultimately they will abandon me.

Reflect on Your Behavior to See What Causes You to Act as You Do

Besides noticing the difference between your beliefs and attitudes and those of other people, another way to uncover your Organizing Principles is to reflect on your behavior to figure out the beliefs and core issues that cause you to act as you do.

Start with observing the specific things you do routinely. For example, soon after I started therapy I noticed the great lengths I went to in order to avoid emotional pain or even to admit to myself that the pain is there. I found it almost impossible to cry or even to experience the grief and anger I felt about my father's death.

I came to realize that my programming interpreted pain as dangerous; that after my father's death my default programming's primary goal was to take responsibility for myself and my mother and, by extension, everyone else, since my inner world believed it was the only way things could possibly work out because others weren't dependable. My default programming interpreted pain as dangerous based on the belief that if I allowed myself to experience pain, it would distract me from the goal of taking care of everything for everyone.

Gradually, I came to see that it wasn't just pain that my programming interpreted as dangerous; it judged all emotions to be dangerous. I came to recognize that this interpretation caused me to avoid most feelings at any cost. Recognizing this belief led me to uncover my second Organizing Principle: "Painful feelings are dangerous." (The corollary is all feelings have the potential to be painful, so all feelings are dangerous.)

Sometimes a psychological observation will hit home and help you accurately pinpoint and define your Organizing Principles. Early on, my first therapist explained, "The idea that we can have control is an illusion, even though we maintain the idea that things can be controlled." Examples are planning to play basketball or golf and being rained out; trying to start your car and discovering your battery has died. Anything can happen to negate what you believe is controllable. But, as my therapist pointed out, that doesn't mean that some of us don't attempt to be in control.

The desire for control often works on an unconscious level. Some years ago I went to a UCLA management seminar. It started with the instructor having 100 of us take a personality test. After he reviewed our tests, he called the names of twelve people and asked them to step out of the room to participate in an exercise. He explained to the rest of us that the twelve were chosen based on their tests. He identified six of them as "controlling types" and the other six as passive types who did not want to be in control. He told us all twelve would be brought back into the class and divided into two teams, one made up of those with "control issues," the other with "non-control issues." The teams would have a competition in which they would be asked to construct a rocket ship out of Legos.

The instructor predicted that each of the controlling people would immediately grab something to establish his or her "control": Perhaps one would pick up the box of Legos or the instructions and another the tools, each of the six unconsciously believing an action would give him or her control. He predicted that the non-controlling people would do the opposite because they would not want to offend the others. He also predicted that the non-controlling people would waste a lot of time organizing themselves because none of them would want to take charge and that it would be just the opposite with the other group. He brought the people back into the room and told them about the game of building the Lego rocket ship without letting them know how and why they were chosen to be on the team to which they were assigned. It was amazing to see that each group acted exactly as he had predicted!

The point of this exercise was that even though the instructor could identify from their personality tests who was a controlling type and who was a non-controlling type, the people themselves didn't necessarily realize they were controlling or non-controlling. The controlling types didn't see grabbing the box, the instructions, or the tools as attempting to be in control; they just did what seemed natural to them. If you asked them why they approached the task the way they did, they might answer, "Because I like to get right down to business" or "Because it was the efficient way to do it."

I had not consciously known how important an issue control was to me until my therapist talked to me about it. I saw that I tried hard to take control of myself and my emotions. I also saw that I tried hard to take control of situations, and that most of the time I did this by trying to dominate the situation.

I started asking myself, "Why is being in control so important to me?" Gradually another question occurred to me: "Do I believe I need to be in control to be safe?" I saw that the answer was yes. The anxiety I experienced often came from a fear that I was losing control and that I would end up being exposed to something I feared, whereas my programming's interpretation was that if I was in control I could get what I needed. With this insight, I realized that another of my Organizing Principles is "I must stay in control to be safe."

How Organizing Principles and Acts Are Related

The more clearly I understood my Organizing Principles, the more clearly I saw how they relate to my acts. For example, my Organizing Principle "I'm not qualified to handle painful situations. That takes a real adult, and in my inner world I'm still a vulnerable kid" is the basis for my act, "Poor me, the boy whose father died when I was eleven, who needs your help, and you're bad if you don't help me."

My Organizing Principle "I must stay in control to be safe" is integrally tied to another act I developed, "You can't stop me if I think I'm right," which I go into to take control of a situation. (I named this act after my belief "You can't stop me if I think I'm right," which I described in Chapter 4 as coming from my childhood experience of opening the door of our moving car so I could free the strap of my portable radio, flying out onto the highway and surviving.) My Organizing Principle "The world isn't safe; don't trust" is also tied to my "You can't stop me if I'm right" act because it's the belief that I can't trust the world to be safe that makes me try to seize control.

The last Organizing Principle on my list, "I'm a good guy and I never hurt anyone unjustly," is the basis for another of my acts, "Mr. Cleanhands," which tells people that I'm a good guy who did nothing wrong (and, therefore, I shouldn't be thrown out of the tribe). Unfortunately, this act robs me of the ability to hear other people, specifically to learn about hurts and problems that I might be responsible for, albeit inadvertently, and to grow as a result of their feedback.

Like our acts, our Organizing Principles can be inconsistent and in conflict with each other. When they are, if we allow them to operate on automatic, they can trap us in a bind that offers no escape and blocks progress toward our goals. For example, my Organizing Principle "Eventually, loving others will make things work out" states that no matter how painful the situation, if I hang in there and keep loving the other person, I'll finally get the love and closeness I crave. But this belief is in direct conflict with "The world isn't safe; don't trust," "No one will take care of my needs but me," and "If they really loved me, they'd never put me in an uncomfortable position."

How can I be close to anyone if I don't trust them, if I feel they can never take care of my needs, and that if they loved me, they'd never ask me to do something that makes me uncomfortable? These beliefs confine me to mistrusting the very people I want to love and want to love me. These beliefs also confine me to seeing my own discomfort in a situation as being the other person's responsibility instead of my own! With these Organizing Principles, it's no wonder that I longed for closeness without experiencing what I craved.

The Interplay between Mindful Awareness and the Brain as "Anticipation Machine"

Let's look at what's happening in our brains when we operate on automatic pilot that allows our Organizing Principles to run us, no matter how dysfunctional these beliefs may be and how disabling a bind they create for us. Because of the brain's very nature and structure, we are programmed to *react*. That's what we do: We constantly react to everything in our life because our brain is set up to scan, monitor, and evaluate the world in order to anticipate future outcomes of current situations and to respond according to its evaluation.

As Daniel Siegel, M.D., explains it, the brain is "an anticipation machine" structured to take experiences that happened in the past and use them to come up with expectations about what will happen in the future.[1] This means that "prior learning shapes present perceptions."[2]

It's important to note that in this context the word *learning* doesn't imply that the "learning" is necessarily accurate knowledge. It just means that what the mind has learned from the past—including our self-defeating Organizing Principles—has become hardwired in our brains. When you're on automatic, it's this prior learning, your *programming*, that determines how you experience what's happening right now and what you anticipate for the future.

When your brain functions on automatic pilot, neuroscientists refer to the process as being *"top-down."*[3] As Siegel explains it, when your brain is functioning top-down, "prior learning will enslave incoming data." When this happens, the past keeps you from experiencing the present because it keeps you from really being *in* the present![4]

This is why your Organizing Principles can trigger inappropriate and dysfunctional behavior. After all, how could your actions in the moment be appropriate and serve you if they are based on mistaken, past-based interpretations?

Top-down functioning isn't just a theoretical way to label what happens in your brain. It actually describes a physiological process. Here's how it works.

The cortex—the neural tissue that covers a large part of the brain—has six layers, each of which is as thick as a business card.[5] Input (information) from the five senses and other direct experience of the present situation comes in through the sixth layer at the bottom (Siegel calls this "bottom-up" input) and goes up to the fifth layer. Top-down input from prior learning comes down from the first and second layers.

At the third and fourth layers, data from the past—your mind's anticipations, judgments, and expectations, including its underlying beliefs that I refer to as your Organizing Principles—comes down and crashes into data from the present that's coming up, and this is where, when you're on automatic pilot, the top-down data enslaves the data that's coming in from the current situation so that "you don't see the present clearly."[6]

Let's say you're in a room where a piece of instrumental music is playing. With a bottom-up experience, you hear the melody, the rhythm, the tone, and the unique sounds of each of the instruments in harmony or in counterpoint. At first you take in the music (the input) with your sense of hearing, but the melody, rhythm, and tone may be so engaging and moving that you start to feel the music in your body. You might even start to dance. You are experiencing the music moment by moment as you hear it.

In contrast, with a top-down experience, while the music is playing you might think about other versions of the piece that you've heard before or other pieces you've heard by the same composer or different composers. You might judge this version of the piece against other versions or other pieces of music and think about which you like better. Or you might think about something else entirely, such as work that you didn't complete at the office or a date that you hope to make for the weekend.

The point is that with top-down experience, you are not in the moment with the music because other data takes dominance over your experience of the music. You *cannot* experience the melody, rhythm, tone, or performance of the music in and of itself because what you're experiencing is being controlled by top-down data that's interfering with a direct experience of the music in the present.[7]

Here's a firsthand example of how one of my Organizing Principles—part of my prior learning—can dominate and control my experience of the present.

Let's say I've gone out socially with a new friend whom I want to connect with. If I'm being mindful, input from what's occurring in the moment will enter from the sixth layer of my cortex and continue going up without crashing into my interpretations and judgments from past experiences. I will be fully present in the moment to enjoy the other person's company, be grateful, and be appropriately responsive.

By contrast, just as we saw in the preceding illustration of a top-down experience of music, my Organizing Principle "The world isn't safe; don't trust" will keep me in the past instead of the present, and I'll be wary, I'll pause, and I'll hold back. My mistrustful Organizing Principle will cause me to be self-protective, and even though consciously I truly want to connect with the other person, I might act indifferent. I might act indifferent for only a moment, but it may be enough to turn a potentially loving situation into an awkward one.

This is a vivid reminder of how our Organizing Principles and the acts they trigger can trap us in the past and rob us of fulfilling relationships in the present and that they will inevitably do this when we allow our brains to function top-down.

Recognizing my Organizing Principles hasn't made them disappear. At some level, they will always be waiting in the wings to cue me to act on them—if I let them. The way I stop letting my dysfunctional beliefs trigger my actions is to be mindful, so that I can prevent my old hardwiring from determining my behavior.

I keep reminding myself that mindfulness allows me to disengage the top-down data so that input from the present will rise up without being held prisoner by anticipations, judgments, expectations, and emotions from the past. If I'm mindful, these anticipations, judgments, expectations, and emotions won't get their way by exerting their pull because I won't hold on to them.

If I'm mindful, I also won't be controlled by the top-down data I'm unconscious of. Mindfulness "dissolves" the anticipations,

judgments, expectations, and emotions that are in our programming and allows us to experience what is as just "what is," and to
make a choice about how to respond in the present rather than
responding reflexively.[8]

Resolve to Dissolve

Remember: Even when anticipations, judgments, expectations, and
past-based emotions arise, the experience of being in the moment
empowers you to make the mindful choice to dissolve them—
not forever, but *in that moment*. Every time you do this, you are
strengthening your ability to be mindful more often.

I think of dissolving my Organizing Principles and other judgments and interpretations that pass through my head as "manually
overriding" them. It's the same process I've referred to as interrupting your machinery. By making the effort to interrupt your machinery and manually override the old beliefs that are an integral part
of your judgments and interpretations, you're giving yourself the
opportunity to choose how you will act instead of mindlessly letting
your hardwiring make that choice for you. You're giving yourself the
opportunity to own your default programming instead of letting
it own you. You're empowering yourself to make conscious, intentional, productive choices about your life.

Please note that I said, "by making the *effort*." Being mindful
requires effort, especially at first. In order to dissolve old beliefs and
judgments, you have to develop the *resolve* to be mindful as much
as possible in your daily life.

More and more, when I feel my Organizing Principles starting to exert their pull, I remind myself that I don't want to be

imprisoned by the past, and I start mindfully paying attention. I monitor the voice in my head when it echoes these old beliefs, and I observe the feelings that are triggered in association with them.

I recognize them as my default programming, created in response to childhood hurts and misinterpretations of past experiences that I allowed to run my life. Every time I'm mindful, my brain is allowing me to experience the present and to respond authentically in the present. Little by little, even though they'll always be in my programming, I'm letting go of my acts and the dysfunctional underlying beliefs that they're based on. In the process, I'm remodeling my brain and transforming my life.

An image that's helped me to see the power that all of us have to let go of our dysfunctional beliefs is to think of ourselves as living in our own unique virtual realities. It's like being the creator, or god, of and in our own universe, one that we created entirely by ourselves, much as an artist fills in a blank canvas with paint.

Each of our universes or virtual realities is different from all others in its details because it is personally programmed through our unique interpretations of our individual experiences. Our machinery builds stories around our relationships and a million other things we encounter in our lives, and these stories—these interpretations and judgments—become our programming, part of the virtual universe that we live in and are creating, even if we don't realize we're creating it.

If you don't like the meaning you are giving your life through the story you are telling yourself, change the story to one you do like. If you don't like the interpretations, judgments, and beliefs that are part of your programming and that determine your experience, change them! Remember, all of us are gods in our own universe!

······· **PAUSE YOUR MACHINERY** ·······

- Think mindfully about your Organizing Principles and write a brief description of each one. For example if one of your underlying beliefs is that it's up to you to solve problems for others, your Organizing Principle might be "I need to take care of anybody who is needy or in pain." If your belief is the opposite—that you need others to take care of your needs and alleviate your pain—your Organizing Principle might be "I can't take care of my own needs, and I'm dependent on other people's help."
- To help you recognize the Organizing Principles that you believe in, think about the following and write down your responses:
  - What do you believe about yourself, and how do you see your place in the world? Do you view yourself in positive terms or in negative terms? How would you describe your overall belief about yourself?
  - When you meet people for the first time, do you have an expectation as to how they will respond to you?
  - Do you expect people close to you to understand you?
  - When you approach a challenge, do you assume you will be able to accomplish it?

- Review the Organizing Principles you've listed and reflect on the ways that they affect your behavior and whether they help you get your needs met or hurt you. Write down your observations about how acting on them helps you or hurts you in getting your needs met.

Now let's look at what recent discoveries about the brain teach us about transforming ourselves so that instead of being governed by old beliefs that sabotage us we can act in ways that will bring us greater fulfillment.

CHAPTER NINE

WHAT BRAIN SCIENCE TEACHES ABOUT HOW TO CHANGE YOUR WIRING TO IMPROVE YOUR LIFE

····· 🧠 ·····

Okay. Now that you've discerned the acts and Organizing Principles that have been running you, you'll always remind yourself to be mindful so you can be in the present, right? No, not really.

It's hard work to remodel your brain and transform your behavior. Your machinery has been entrenching in your mind the belief system you've been developing in your programming for as long as you've been alive, and this isn't going to shift easily.

Learning to be mindful and not to be run by your default programming is a *continuing process*. After you've started to recognize, interrupt, and let go of your old programming, your machinery—which, in terms of the brain, includes your amygdala, the part of your central nervous system that sends out fear signals—will still be there, waiting to kidnap your "control center" and take you over if you let it. This is its job and, as we've seen, in issues like driving and avoiding accidents we're blessed by it; in relationships and many other situations, sometimes we're not!

That's why it's crucial to remember to reflect mindfully on your thoughts and actions. When you realize you've acted on automatic pilot and in a self-defeating way, with your new mindfulness you can view yourself and your actions with the COAL qualities of curiosity, openness, acceptance, and love rather than judging yourself for the very fact that you are human.

The process of becoming more mindful requires committing to the goal of mindfulness and, equally importantly, to the effort it takes to be mindful, and not condemning yourself for being human and sometimes acting mindlessly.

Up to now, I've presented in broad strokes information I've learned about the brain that's helped me understand the relationship between how our brains develop and function and how we can remodel our brains to transform ourselves. Now I'd like to share some additional information about scientists' discoveries about the brain that has made me understand exactly why I can still find myself operating dysfunctionally at times and why self-transformation is an endlessly continuing process.

This information has deepened my understanding of how my early experiences shaped both my mind and my brain, and why they continue to play such a significant role in shaping who I am as an adult. It's taught me why I need to develop the capacity to be flexible, adaptive, coherent, energized, and stable (the FACES qualities I discussed in Chapter 7). It's encouraged me to be loving and compassionate with myself when I realize that I've acted mindlessly, and it's strengthened my commitment to being mindful.

As I mentioned in Chapter 5, as we're growing up we develop templates that help us modulate the responses of our amygdala. Research has revealed that early experiences have a specific impact on abilities related to the region of the brain that allows us to modulate ourselves mentally, emotionally, and physically,[1] all of which are necessary to our being able to be in the moment, to recognize our acts, to dis-identify with the voice in our head, and to disengage from our Organizing Principles and the dysfunctional acts they trigger. Most importantly, research has also revealed more about what we can do to improve our ability to modulate ourselves in these vital areas so that we increase our enjoyment of life and have a greater sense of well-being.

Where It All Begins: The Healthy Functioning of Your Prefrontal Cortex

As you know from Chapter 5, the cerebral cortex is the part of the brain that gives you your higher cognitive functions (language, logic, and planning). It modulates the primitive emotional responses of your limbic system, including those of your brain's fear center, the amygdala, and your reptilian complex, which regulates fight or flight. Your cerebral cortex also monitors and influences the neural network in the rest of your body.

The *middle prefrontal cortex*, located behind the forehead, is crucial in providing these abilities. Summarizing research on this region of the brain, Daniel Siegel, M.D., explains that the prefrontal cortex has long neurons that extend to different parts of the brain and the entire body, and this enables the process of *integration*, which he says is "the underlying common mechanism beneath various pathways leading to well-being."[2] He lists nine *"executive functions"* that the middle prefrontal cortex participates in.[3] As you read this list, think about how you are functioning in these areas and whether you would like to improve in one or more of them.

1. Regulating your body (vital organs such as your heart and other bodily systems to keep them in balance)

2. Attuned communication with other people

3. Emotional balance (monitoring and influencing the limbic system, including the amygdala and reptilian complex, and also monitoring the body, so that you experience your life as emotionally stimulating but not so much so that it's overwhelming or that you close down emotionally)

4. Response flexibility (taking in information, stopping, and reflecting before you act)

5. Insight (seeing the workings of your own mind, the ability to reflect on the past and connect it in a productive way to the present and with your projections of the future)

6. Empathy ("seeing" and resonating with the minds of others by imagining what it's like to experience the world from their point of view)

7. Modulating fear (the capacity to soothe the amygdala to quiet the machinery when fear is not the appropriate response)

8. Being in touch with intuition (openness to the wisdom that your body and "being" can communicate to you about what is happening inside you and what your nervous system picks up from resonating with others)

9. Morality (feeling deep compassion for and connectedness to others and wanting to act for the higher good).[4]

Now that you've read this list, you see why healthy functioning of your middle prefrontal cortex is necessary for a sense of well-being. These nine functions enable you to modulate yourself mentally, emotionally, and physically. If you believe that your functioning is less than optimal in any of these areas, you now know that part of remodeling your brain means that you'll be remodeling your middle prefrontal cortex.

Parent-Child Attachments and the Middle Prefrontal Cortex

Scientists' findings about the value of a healthy middle prefrontal cortex are only part of what they've discovered about this crucial part of the brain. Another fascinating fact is that the first seven of the functions of the middle prefrontal cortex (regulating your body, attuned communication, emotional balance, response flexibility, insight, empathy, and modulating fear) are also outcomes of a secure relationship between parent and child during the first few years of a child's life.[5]

The more attuned a parent is to his or her young child, the safer the child will feel; the more secure the bond between parent and child will be; and the healthier the child's development will be in the first seven areas the middle prefrontal cortex participates in that enable us to modulate ourselves mentally, emotionally, and physically. Thus, parents who are mindful in their relationships with their children provide secure attachments. As Siegel puts it, "COAL [curious, open, accepting, loving] is exactly what parents who provide secure attachment to their children have as a stance toward their kids."[6] Conversely, because of a parent's own genetic background, childhood traumas, current issues, and lack of self-understanding, the more that parent is what I've referred to as a "wire monkey" parent, the less mindful the parent will be, the less safe the child will feel, the less secure the parent-child attachment will be, and the less healthily developed these seven functions will be for the child starting in childhood and going into adulthood.

This finding helps us understand what I discussed in Chapter 2 about ruptures in emotional attachment being traumatic for children, and why it is that if less than around 50 percent of such ruptures are repaired for a child soon after the event, the child won't have received what psychologists refer to as "good enough" attunement from the parent (or parents). That lack of good enough attunement is likely to have a destructive effect on the child's development in at least some areas, including self-image, self-confidence, self-knowledge, and ability to accomplish goals.

If one or both of your parents, due to their own biology, backgrounds, and experiences, were unable to be sufficiently attuned to you to create a secure parent-child attachment, you're bound to be experiencing less than optimal functioning in one or more of the seven abilities promoted by secure parent-child attachments.

- Maybe in certain situations your heart has a tendency to beat too fast or your intestines churn too much (problems regulating your body).
- Maybe you have a hard time tuning in to other people's feelings, resonating with them enough to understand what they feel, what they want, even what they may be trying to tell you (problems with attuned communication).

- Maybe it's difficult for you to modulate your emotions and instead you feel your emotions are taking you on a roller-coaster ride or that you don't feel your emotions at all, that you simply can't see why feelings are such a "big deal" (problems with emotional balance).

- Maybe you can't stop yourself from acting impulsively and you find it difficult to weigh different options and choose the most appropriate ones (problems with response flexibility).

- Maybe you find it hard to reflect on your past to see what it tells you that's actually applicable to the present or future and what is not (problems with insight).

- Maybe it's difficult for you to put yourself in the place of others, to imagine what it would be like to look at the world from their perspective (problems with empathy).

- Maybe it's hard to monitor and calm down your fear when it would be helpful to do so (problems with modulating fear).

All of these are related to the functioning of your middle prefrontal cortex, and healthy functioning in these areas is associated with secure parent-child relationships. (Many believe that the eighth and ninth executive functions—being in touch with intuition and morality—may also be promoted by secure parent-child relationships, but the research hasn't been done yet to test his hypothesis.)[7]

How the Mind's Regulation of the Flow of Energy and Information Affects Relationships

Why would the healthy development of at least seven of the nine functions of the middle prefrontal cortex also be outcomes of a secure parent-child attachment? Because, as we learned from Siegel, the mind is an "embodied and relational process of regulating the flow of energy and information,"[8] which means that our relationships are an integral part of the way our mind moves energy and information in our brain, and the specific ways in which energy and information move in our brain influence the way our brain develops and functions. Thus, starting at birth, our relationships have a profound influence on the sculpting and functioning of our brain.

The way it works is this: The mind regulates energy and information flow within ourselves and shares it with others through our neural circuitry, which is constantly responding to people we encounter as theirs is responding to us. The pathways along which this energy and information flows become embedded in our brains.[9]

Babies and young children need others for survival: They are dependent on their parents and other caregivers and are naturally open in sharing energy and information with them. Since the flow of energy and information along a baby's and a young child's neural network is creating neural pathways, the security or lack of security of the relationship between parent and child—in other words, the security or lack of security of a parent-child attachment—impacts the formation of the neural pathways that become embedded in their young brain. This includes the neural pathways in the middle prefrontal cortex, of course, which affect at least seven of the nine executive functions.[10] This is the process by which "early experience shapes the structure and the function of the brain."[11]

When relationships between parent and child are "attuned," a child feels it and experiences a sense of stability in the present moment. During that here-and-now interaction, the child feels good, connected, and loved. The child's internal world is seen with clarity by the parent, and the parent comes to resonate with the child's state. This is attunement.[12]

Over time, this attuned communication enables the child to develop the regulatory circuits in the brain—including the integrative prefrontal fibers—that give the child a source of resilience as he or she grows. This resilience, which comes from "secure attachment," includes the capacity for self-regulation and engaging with others in empathetic relationships. As I've discussed, the others of the first seven executive functions have been demonstrated to be outcomes of secure attachment as well.[13]

I gained further clarity about the ways that early experiences shape our brains from a *New York Times* article by naturalist Diane Ackerman. In it she reports that brain scans have allowed scientists to observe a synchronicity between the brains of a mother and child, and that advances in neuroimaging have shown that an infant's first attachments actually imprint the brain.[14]

According to Ackerman, there is scientific evidence of the importance of loving touch, one of the fundamental elements of a secure parent-child attachment. She explains that we can see its beneficial effects through an experiment in which adults in a loving relationship were given an electrical shock that produced pain. It had a lower neural reaction in their brains when they were holding a loving partner's hand than when they were not holding it. Researchers did not find this response in people holding a partner's hand if the relationship between the partners was unharmonious. Ackerman also reports that holding a loving partner's hand can lower blood pressure, improve health, soothe physical pain, and ease reaction to stress.[15]

The effects of rejection on the brain are dramatic in the opposite way. Neuroimaging studies show that "the same areas of the brain that register physical pain are active when someone feels socially rejected," Ackerman says. "That's why being spurned by a lover hurts all over the body, but in no place you can point to. Or rather, you'd need to point to the dorsal anterior cingulate cortex in the brain . . . the bundle of nerve fibers zinging messages between the hemispheres that register both rejection and physical assault."[16]

Comparing how a loving touch affects the brain with how rejection affects it, we get a deeper understanding of the ways in which a parent's attunement to a baby and the security or lack of security of the parent-child attachment imprints a baby's brain, thereby affecting at least seven of the nine executive functions that are crucial to our sense of well-being and our having harmonious relationships. As Ackerman puts it, the imprinting from an infant's first attachments begins patterns of thinking, behavior, self-image, and choices about intimate relationships that carry through into adulthood.[17]

These findings needn't discourage you, however. As you know from our discussion about the brain's malleability, neuroscientist Richard Davidson is right to emphasize that the emotional style from childhood that takes us into our lives as adults "doesn't need to be the one that describes us forever."[18] If you didn't have a secure parent-child relationship growing up and you'd like to increase your ability with one or more of the seven executive functions that are affected by the nature of the parenting you experienced, you can accomplish this by remodeling your brain.

Before sharing with you another way to think about this remodeling process that's proven valuable to me, and discussing techniques you can use to support you in the process of remodeling your brain, I'd like you to Pause Your Machinery, reflect on the information you've just read and see how it applies to you and what it tells you about your specific goals for self-transformation.

PAUSE YOUR MACHINERY

- Let's begin this slightly longer section of Pause Your Machinery for this chapter with an exercise to help you get additional insight into your early childhood experiences. Our goal is to look into the causes of your parents' attunement or lack of attunement to you. Think mindfully about the factors that created your parents' default programming and write a description of them.
  - What were your grandparents like?
  - How did they impact your mother and father?
  - Were there major traumas in either or both of your parents' early lives? If so, what were they?
- If your parents are alive, you may want to interview them in a mindful way, by which I mean to stay in the present, with curiosity, openness, acceptance, and love, and to listen without judgment and without shaming and blaming. If possible, you might also interview a sibling or a childhood friend of the relevant parent.
- When you have as much information as you can gather, write a description of your mother's and your father's youth experience,

including the most impactful emotional events, the type of parenting each had, and the belief system each downloaded from his or her parents (or developed in reaction to his or her parents).

- Describe in writing your parents' fears, how much you believe their fear(s) controlled them, and what you believe their Organizing Principles were. Describe the defenses they developed in response to the pain they experienced. Once you have described these factors, you have described your parents' default programming.

- Now describe the way you think your mother's and your father's programming affected their parenting of you. Write down whether you feel that they were mindful, nurturing parents some or much of the time or that they were "wire monkey parents" functioning on automatic pilot most or all of the time.

- If you find yourself experiencing anger at them for areas in which you feel that they parented you inadequately, review your description of their most emotionally impactful childhood experiences and of how their programming affected their parenting of you. Does your knowledge of the traumas that created their programming make you feel that at some point you will be able to feel compassion and possibly empathy for them for what they experienced in childhood? Do you feel empathy for yourself for what you experienced as a child?

For the first part of this exercise, you've looked into the past for insight into how it is affecting the present. In the next part, you'll reflect on the present for clues as to how you want to transform yourself today in order to create a more fulfilling tomorrow.

- Reflecting on the information about your parents that you've gathered in the first half of this Pause Your Machinery exercise, how do you feel your parents' attunement or lack of attunement to you during your childhood affects you today? Do you feel that you're functioning less than optimally in any of the first seven executive functions that are outcomes of secure parent-child attachment and of healthy development of the middle prefrontal cortex (regulating your body, attuned communication, emotional balance, response flexibility, insight, empathy, and modulating fear)? If so, list the areas in which you would like to function better.

- Next to each area you listed as being one in which you would like to function better, write a description of how you function in that area now and why you feel that it's less than optimal. Then describe how you would like to function in that area.

- Compare this list with what you've written in response to earlier Pause Your Machinery exercises about ways you've acted on automatic pilot and how they've been dysfunctional (the exercises at the ends of Chapters 1 and 3); about your acts and what they've cost you (the exercise at the end of Chapter 7); and your Organizing Principles and the ways they've hurt you (the exercise at the end of Chapter 8). Do you see a relationship between your dysfunctional behaviors and beliefs and the executive function(s) that you would like to improve? If so, describe which area you feel that the beliefs and behavior are related to. For example, in problems with relationships—such as feeling that you're being judged, shamed, and blamed and easily becoming activated and angry or feeling too fearful of losing a relationship to stand up for yourself—the problems may be related to attuned communication, emotional balance, response flexibility, insight, empathy, and modulating fear.

As with all your written exercises, keep what you've just written for reference. It will give you insight into your default programming and provide you with objectives for remodeling your brain to improve your functioning in the areas that will help you create a happier experience of life.

In the next chapter, I'll share with you how you can remodel your brain by parenting yourself with mindful awareness.

CHAPTER TEN

PARENTING YOURSELF THROUGH PRACTICING MINDFULNESS

..... 🧠 .....

I talked about parenting yourself in connection with the process of dis-identifying with the judgmental voice in your head and disengaging from your "acts." Parenting yourself will result in making intentional choices that support transformation in the way that an attuned parent guides and supports a child to grow into a healthy, fully functioning adult. I learned to parent myself when I was in therapy with Robin L. Kay, Ph.D., who taught me that parenting yourself means treating yourself with the caring, love, and compassion you would have for a young child you love. The essential component of parenting yourself is mindful awareness.

Studies have demonstrated that the nine executive functions that create a sense of well-being and are associated with the middle prefrontal cortex are also outcomes of practicing mindful awareness.[1] Research shows as well that the more we practice mindfulness intentionally, the more mindful we will tend to be.[2] Thus, the more we mindfully parent ourselves, the more we will improve our nine executive functions, the easier it will be for us to be mindful in the future, and the more we will increase our sense of well-being because we will be increasingly able to modulate ourselves mentally, emotionally, and physically. In other words, the more we practice mindfulness, the more that mindfulness will become a new "habit" that replaces dysfunctional mental and behavioral habits with healthier ways of thinking and acting.

How to Cultivate Mindful Awareness

The prerequisite for us to learn to parent ourselves is to cultivate mindful awareness. In the following section, I'll share with you techniques that will help you do this.

Mindfulness Meditation

Studies on the constructive effects of mindful awareness have been conducted on people who took *mindfulness-based stress reduction* classes, which taught them to develop the trait of mindful awareness through *mindfulness meditation*.[3] Mindfulness meditation, or insight meditation, are the English terms for a type of Buddhist meditation known as *Vipassana*,[4] "an analytical method based on mindfulness, awareness, vigilance, observation."[5] As you can see from this description, practicing mindfulness meditation *is* practicing mindful awareness. During mindfulness meditation, when judgments and other thoughts come up, you observe and vigilantly let go of them, using mindfulness to dissolve them in the moment so that you can be in the present and be open to a direct experience of the here and now.

Perhaps the most common mindfulness meditation is one that teaches you to do this by sitting in a comfortable position, on a chair or on the floor, with your back straight and your eyes closed, and focusing on your breath. In addition to this type of practice, Daniel Siegel, M.D., points out that yoga, qi gong, tai chi, and the Christian practice of centered prayer are also forms of mindfulness meditation.[6]

Over a number of years, I experimented with various meditation techniques I learned in classes and seminars or from books, and I called upon them in times of frustration, personal crisis, or pain. Three years ago I began a consistent practice of mindfulness meditation by focusing on my breath, and now I practice that four or five times a week.

In Part IV I'll share with you more precise instructions for mindfulness meditations. For now, as you think about the idea of beginning to practice a type of mindfulness meditation, it's important to know that closing your eyes and focusing on your breath doesn't mean that the activity of your mind will suddenly stop. It can feel awkward and challenging not to judge yourself for the mental chatter that continually arises, but I've learned that as long as I keep returning my attention to the breath, gradually a sense of calmness and an ability to focus on being in the present will appear.

Not holding on to thoughts and not judging yourself for having thoughts *is* the practice, because dissolving thoughts and judgments and using your intention to return your attention to the breath in the present moment is being mindful.

You don't need to practice mindfulness meditation to develop mindfulness, however. You can practice and develop mindfulness just by doing everyday things mindfully.[7] This means, for any activity you do, being present with curiosity, openness, acceptance, and love; experiencing the activity moment to moment, without seizing and holding on to whatever judgments, expectations, memories, and other thoughts pass through your mind.

When you do this, you're not only having a mindful experience of that activity, you're practicing mindfulness, which will help you develop the trait of being mindful in your everyday life instead of acting on automatic pilot. You can change a child's diaper mindfully, hang up clothes in your closet mindfully, prepare a meal mindfully, vacuum or dust the house mindfully, exercise mindfully, do a creative activity mindfully. You can do any activity mindfully just by *being present for it*, not holding on to your mental chatter but instead intentionally focusing your mind on the present to be in the moment, experiencing the activity.

Other Ways to Develop a State of Mindfulness

In hindsight, I now see that running was the first activity that put me in a state of mindfulness. I began to run when I was in my twenties. Everyone was doing it, and, having grown up as a chubby kid and still bearing the scars of feeling stigmatized by it, I thought running seemed a good way to stay fit.

It wasn't long before I was running six days a week, and now, more than forty years later, I'm still doing it. Traditionally, running isn't thought of as a meditative practice, but for me it has been. I've found that running creates the space for mindfulness by focusing my mind on the present and disengaging me from my machinery. When I run, I can't keep a train of thought for more than a few seconds. My mental chatter starts to flit from thing to thing, and eventually dissolves so that I become fully absorbed in what I am experiencing in the moment: seeing the trees by the roadside and the cars speeding by; the feel of the breeze on my skin, my body sweating; the muscles in my legs tensing and relaxing as I raise and lower my legs to run; my feet pounding the grassy path beneath them; my lungs expanding as they fill with air and contracting as I expel it, the air I breathe cool and clean in winter and warm and sweet in the summer.

All in all, the net result is that the act of running frees up the stranglehold of my machinery's past-based agendas, allowing me to be mindful of experiencing running in the moment.

Oil painting has also become an activity that has added to my ability to be mindful. It demands my mind to focus on a task, which allows me to be in the moment, thereby creating a state of mindfulness. While painting, as with running, other thoughts enter my mind—memories, to-do lists, business issues, relationship issues, judgments about whether I'm painting well or badly—but I let go of them as I focus on being present in the process of painting, which always brings me back into the moment. (It's very similar to focusing on my breath.)

As with running, I didn't start painting in order to practice mindfulness, but it has become a mindfulness practice. I've come to see that in addition to creating a mental sanctuary that allows creativity to flow through me, connecting me with the collective unconscious, painting is part of my process of practicing mindfulness and parenting myself.

Parenting Yourself Will Improve Your Executive Functions

Parenting yourself with mindfulness can help you improve some of the nine executive functions you learned about in Chapter 9. As examples, let's look specifically at empathy and modulating fear.

Empathy

As you know, if your parents were highly critical of you when you were a child, your programming is likely to include a highly judgmental and vocal inner critic. But that's not the only way you can develop this trait. Although neither of my parents was highly critical of me, even before my father died I grew up with a sense of dis-ease in my family, a sense that something was wrong. And at some deep unconscious level, I believed that the something that was wrong was me, and I developed a strong inner critic in myself, which fed the other three common negative beliefs: *I'm not good enough; I don't belong here;* and *I'm always going to be on my own.* Perceiving the world from this perspective, I magnified whatever my parents said to me that might be construed as a criticism, and I started making a mental list of what I considered to be my faults.

If, like me, you find yourself frequently criticizing and judging yourself, then you're not relating to yourself with enough empathy, and you need to parent yourself to learn to develop empathy. I received a highly critical email the other day from a friend. Without thinking, my machinery automatically reacted by siding with his position and piling criticism onto myself. Within the next few minutes, I began to look mindfully at what was really going on with me. I came to see that I was not responding with any empathy for myself but instead was going back to my default position, which contains a lot of old, unnecessary negative feelings about and evaluations of myself that just didn't apply in this situation. This made the clouds part, and I could see that my friend just had a different perception from mine and I didn't need to be mean to myself. Both his perception and mine could coexist peacefully.

Applying the process of developing empathy for other people, according to Siegel, can help you develop empathy for yourself.[8] Empathy involves other executive functions as well, including attuned communication and insight. The more you mindfully work on feeling empathy for others, the more you improve your attuned communication with them and with yourself, and therefore increase your insight into yourself. Thus all of these capacities can grow out of mindfully engaging in the process of developing empathy.

Modulating Fear

As I've mentioned, for years I had a fear of my anger because embedded in my programming was the belief that it was dangerous and, therefore, "bad," and I shouldn't allow myself to feel it. Unexpectedly, one of my experiences with painting gave me information that I was able to apply mindfully to help me modulate my fear of anger. Here's how it happened.

For seven years, I participated in a class at UCLA on creativity for artists. The class was open by invitation to artists from all genres of art, including the visual arts, writing, and music. The two professors who taught the class had Ph.D.s in psychology. One specialized in anthropology, the other in issues of deafness.

Each week's three-hour class was divided into two sessions, with one participant in each session sharing the details of a recent dream and, under the guidance of the professors, the other members of the class analyzing the dream by asking question after question based on associations with details in the dreams.

During one class, I shared a long and intricate dream in which I was being chased by "bad guys." In one particular snippet, I was terrified and looking for a safe place when I knocked on a stranger's door, asking to be taken in for safety. A kind woman—no one I recognized—opened her door and displayed empathy but refused me entry. One of the professors suggested that she represented my "dark feminine or shadow [unconscious] side" and asked me to explore the purpose of the dream by making a painting.

For that painting I gave myself permission to let it simply evolve as intuitions showed up. What evolved was a self-portrait that was split down the center of my head and torso, with the left side being me as a male and the right side as a female.

The main realization that came to me out of nowhere was this understanding: Until I did that self-portrait, my inner world believed that if I ever let my anger unleash itself on my friends and family, I was capable of blowing them away, so I had always been careful to keep it in check. While painting my male and female sides, I came to recognize that I would never let that rage out offensively in a destructive way; I would only let it surface to defend myself. Coupled with the mindfulness I was developing in therapy, I realized I don't have to be afraid that my anger will hurt people; I know that allowing my anxiety to cover up my anger only hurts me. If I start feeling anxious about getting angry, I mindfully recognize it's my programming that's cueing the anxiety, I tell myself that it's okay for me to feel angry, and I allow myself to feel the anger.

Learning from the process of painting the self-portrait that I don't need to be afraid of my anger, and developing the ability to disempower my fear, fits into Siegel's description of how fears become triggered in the brain, the way the brain can modulate fear, and why mindfulness helps us to modulate it.

Once a terrifying experience has become embedded in your amygdala, it creates a neural firing pattern that's activated whenever you come into contact with what first terrified you or whatever your mind interprets as being similar to it. Your middle prefrontal cortex can modulate fear by growing fibers that secrete *gamma-amino butyric acid (GABA)*, a neurochemical that calms your fear by inhibiting the secretion of another neurochemical that would stimulate the fear. The secretion of GABA permits you to experience bottom-up data from the present instead of being taken over by your fear that would be triggered by the top-down control of your past experiences.[9]

You can use mindfulness to unlearn fears either in therapy, with the guidance and support of a trained psychotherapist, or by processing the fear with mindful awareness on your own. Mindful awareness permits you to see fear as, as Siegel puts it, "just an activity of the mind" or "just the amygdala firing."[10] Now when I feel fear coming up in circumstances where I recognize that it's inappropriate, I become my own mindful parent: I interrupt my machinery, manually override my programming, and mindfully remind myself that the fear is only an activity of my mind (or just my amygdala firing). I then take a deep breath and keep breathing fully, and I remind myself that using mindfulness to calm down my fear is not only helping me at that moment but also creating changes in my brain that will make it easier for me to modulate fear in the future.

When you use this process—mindfully reminding yourself that inappropriate fear is just the default firing of your amygdala—mindfulness allows you to unlearn fear of cats or dogs, places, activities, situations, and/or emotions that frightened you in the past. It also allows you to recognize that they no longer need to frighten you. The practice of mindful awareness promotes the growth of the integrative middle prefrontal regions, as does "the process of mindful living itself."[11] With some findings to back it up, Siegel hypothesizes that an "effective therapeutic relationship between clinician and patient/client" also promotes the growth of the fibers in this region.[12]

Parenting Yourself to Heal from Painful Memories

Similarly, we can use mindfulness to help overcome pain associated with memories of past traumas. Most of us believe that our memories are similar to films or videotapes of events we've experienced and that when we recall them, they play accurately in our heads and are always exactly the same.[13] But research shows that this isn't the case. What actually happens is that every time we recall a memory, the memory reconsolidates itself in our brains through specific proteins at certain synapses. In fact, each time we remember it, the memory can be slightly different, and it is actually changed by the very act of our remembering it![14]

Research has also shown that the various components of our memories are stored in specific parts of our brain: the visual components in one part, the auditory in another part, and the emotional in the amygdala. The part of a memory that is most vivid to us at a particular time is influenced by our thoughts and feelings at that moment. For example, if we're already feeling sad when a memory comes up, we may remember the sad emotions associated with a memory more than at another time because that element is emphasized when the memory is reconsolidated.

But reconsolidation also opens the door to healing the painful emotions stored in the amygdala.[15] In many such situations, therapy can be healing, and the reason therapy can work has to do with the nature and functioning of our brain and their relationship to memory. "When therapy heals, when it helps reduce the impact of negative memories," neuroscientist Joseph LeDoux explains, "it's really because of reconsolidation . . . Therapy allows people to rewrite their own memories while in a safe space, guided by trained professionals. The difference is that we finally understand the neural mechanism."[16]

A few years ago, a situation in my family was very painful for me. When discussing it with my therapist, she quickly linked the present-day issue that was causing me so much pain with my old memories of my father's passing and my feelings of abandonment. As I've mentioned, when I first went to therapy, the therapist helped me to uncover and feel the pain about my father's death that I'd denied for so long. Now, years later, by recognizing and continuing to process those feelings and to see their relationship to my present-day experiences, I felt the pain in the current situation lessen and some of the pain disappeared from my memory of my father's passing. This is a vivid example of how therapy has helped me to process and heal painful memories.

Parenting Yourself by Giving Yourself a "Time Out"

Research on how the brain works also explains what happens when, as I mentioned in Part I, we encounter something that sets off our machinery and gets us activated so that we go into full battle alert, defending ourselves and/or attacking others. This research explains why, even after we've started becoming more mindful, we're bound to become activated from time to time and how to use parenting ourselves to calm ourselves down.

It's often a highly dramatic state when we're activated, but although we feel very intensely, the emotions we're experiencing so intensely are emotions that are catalyzed by our default programming. In this state, our machinery immediately goes to our Organizing Principles—those old beliefs about ourselves, the world, and our place in it. This process of past-based thinking has the effect of causing our future to look just like our past.

The verb *activated* describes exactly what happens in the brain at such moments. As you know, the amygdala is the part of the brain related to emotion, fear, memory, and aggression, and it responds to what we perceive as threats. According to pediatric neurologist Andrew Curran, research on the brain has demonstrated that the physiological process that occurs when we get activated is that the amygdala receives input via neurochemicals from a system of nerve cells called the *reticular activating system (RAS)*, which goes up through our brain from our spinal cord and governs our state of arousal ranging from sleeping to being highly activated. Simultaneously, the amygdala also responds to our body's release of *adrenaline*, a stress hormone that stimulates our "fight or flight" response and other emotions catalyzed by situations we perceive as threats.[17] "The more excited you are, the more aroused your RAS is, and the higher the level of excitation of your amygdala," Curran explains. "In this state there is often very little conscious mind being used."[18]

This information has helped me understand why, even after years of work to transform myself, there are times when I still continue to act mindlessly when I become activated. I may become so activated—so *un*-present, so *not*-in-the-moment—that I can't hear what another person is really saying. Instead, I hear only what my "listening" tells me he or she is saying, based on my programmed beliefs about what I expect to hear.

Curran explains that the neurochemistry of the amygdala's activation is the basis behind the strategy of "Time Out" with children, calming them down before talking to them about changing their behavior. This same neurochemistry, and consequently, the same strategy, applies to us as adults. "Going toe-to-toe with any individual who has already lost it is only going to wind the situation up further," comments Curran. "Back off, take your time, and calmly contain the situation. Then you may start to get some results."[19]

Once you recognize that you're activated, you will intellectually understand that you're not responding with the higher functions of the cerebral cortex and, therefore, not thinking clearly. When you're in this state, it's *impossible* to be objective about your own behavior and to hear what other people may be telling you.

You have to focus your conscious mind intentionally to interrupt your machinery and to manually override your programming. Give yourself a Time Out, calm yourself down, and, using the higher functions of your cerebral cortex—language, logic, and planning—start to mindfully process what is happening in the moment rather than allowing yourself to be controlled by hardwiring from your past that may lead you to act in ways that are off base.

Calming yourself down after you've been activated by something and mindfully processing your responses is the fundamental first step in transforming yourself by remodeling your brain in regard to the particular trigger for activation. After a Time Out, you can think about your behavior and see which of your old Organizing Principles came into play and which of your acts were triggered. You can also look at the effects that being activated and acting mindlessly had on you and the people with whom you may have been interacting.

A friend recently told me a story about needing a Time Out when driving with his wife to meet another couple for dinner. He thought he knew where the restaurant was but found he was mistaken. He asked his wife to call the restaurant but she hadn't brought her cell phone.

Let me interrupt the story here to share the detail that my friend grew up with a hyper-controlling, critical father. The combination of being late and feeling wrong (combined with the unconscious belief that such "failures" will get him thrown out of the tribe) put him in warp-speed activation.

Although in reality being late wasn't a big deal, my friend had a meltdown, turned the judgment he felt about himself on his wife, and shouted at her for being in the wrong for not bringing her cell phone.

Once he took the Time Out, which allowed him to be mindful about how he'd become activated, totally taken over by his machinery and its old programming, he apologized to his wife, and together they solved the problem of finding the restaurant.

Siegel refers to acting mindlessly in this hyperactivated way as reacting to a "hot-button issue" and "flipping our lid."[20] He emphasizes that by mindfully using the adult version of the Time Out technique during the incident, if possible, and by mindfully reflecting on the incident afterward, as my friend did, you can take responsibility for your actions and repair a rupture in a conversation and a relationship.[21]

This has become my method of parenting myself when I "flip my lid" in response to a "hot-button issue" as I continue on my journey of transformation. I've made it a personal practice to wait at least thirty minutes before responding to texts and emails that can be activating for me. Giving myself a Time Out has saved me from many self-defeating actions.

Again, remember that we as humans are designed to react, react, and react! We have no choice but to react; the trick is to react mindfully. And we cannot react mindfully if we are still activated. When you're activated, parent yourself by giving yourself a Time Out before you react so that you won't react in a thoughtless *and possibly hurtful* manner.

PAUSE YOUR MACHINERY

- Think mindfully about whether there are specific situations or issues that tend to make you activated. If so, list them.

- Write a description of how you feel when these situations or issues come up. Upset? Anxious? Angry? Fearful? Does your default programming make you perceive these situations or issues as a threat? If so, describe how your mind perceives them as threats.

- Write a description of how you act when you become activated in these circumstances and, without shaming or blaming yourself, how your actions affect other people who are with you at the time. Are there specific acts that you go into when you get activated? If so, describe them and describe the circumstances or issues that tend to trigger these acts.

- Reflect mindfully about what experiences in your past may have embedded interpretations in your default programming to cause you to respond as you do when these situations or issues arise. Write a description of the past experiences and how they trigger you to become activated now.

In your daily life, if you observe that you're becoming activated, do your best to take a Time Out. Consider the adage *think before you act*. If you become activated, do your best to interrupt your machinery and, instead of staying on automatic pilot, focus your mind on the present, acknowledge your activated behavior, and take responsibility for it. If you see that you've acted in an inappropriate way that upset or hurt another person, apologize for it. If you remain activated and don't take a Time Out, afterward reflect on what happened, learn from it, and, again, do your best to repair any upset that you may have caused with your inappropriate, activated behavior.

Identifying how your default programming activates you in response to certain situations or issues is a crucial component of parenting yourself. It is the point in the process where you commit to making mindful choices in connection with these triggering situations and issues so that, more and more, you'll make sensible choices in response to them instead of always being at their effect.

Now that you've seen techniques for parenting yourself, take a look in the next chapter at another method I've found effective in helping me to let go of dysfunctional patterns and to support myself in making mindful choices.

CHAPTER ELEVEN

FORMULATING GUIDING PRINCIPLES TO HELP YOU ACT MINDFULLY

..... 🧠 .....

One of my most valuable tools for staying in the present is what I call my *Guiding Principles*. Once I was able recognize my Organizing Principles and see their self-defeating aspects, I began to formulate new Guiding Principles to replace them. These new principles remind me what I've learned about living life without being held captive by my judgments and interpretations and expectations.

You Can Replace Your Old Operating Principles with New Guiding Principles

More and more, when I feel the pull of my old Organizing Principles and the acts they trigger, I interrupt my machinery and mindfully turn to my Guiding Principles.

Let me share with you each of my Guiding Principles and how they strengthen my ability to be mindfully aware.

The truth is just the truth.

This Guiding Principle reminds me that no matter how I interpret a situation, it remains exactly the same. It is the way it is, no matter what I make of it. There is no right and no wrong about it; it just is.

Because of the nature of our brain and mind, we are designed to judge and interpret everything, and to attach meaning and significance to those judgments and interpretations. I've learned that judgments like "good" and "bad," questions like "What if this?" "What if that?" and expectations like "It should be like this" or "It should be like that" are just activities of my mind, which will take me out of the present and create problems for me.

When I interrupt my machinery and remind myself of the Guiding Principle that *the truth is just the truth*, it helps me to dissolve these past-based judgments and interpretations, to stop evaluating and predicting, and to recognize that what is, is just what is. It isn't good or bad; it's just the truth.

When I remind myself that the truth is just the truth, I interrupt my machinery, stop my brain from functioning top-down, and, through mindfulness, bring my brain into functioning bottom-up, which receives incoming data from the present. I experience what is happening in the moment, and I can respond based on what is actually occurring and, therefore, respond more authentically and appropriately.

Remembering that the truth is just the truth helps me in situations every day. For example, if a business deal doesn't go the way I want it to, or if a problem comes up in a personal relationship, when I remember that what is, is just what is, instead of complaining about it, blaming others or myself, I can mindfully reflect on how I want to respond and I can respond in the most constructive way I can.

The Guiding Principle *the truth is just the truth* keeps me in the present and reminds me that what is, is just what is. When we simply state what the truth is, whatever bind our judgments and interpretations create will vanish.

Feelings are not facts.

This Guiding Principle reminds me that no matter how strongly I feel about my point of view, it is still a *feeling*; it's not an objective statement of reality. No matter how intensely I may feel I'm right about something, realizing that feelings are not facts keeps me from being self-righteous, and it allows me to be open to other people's thoughts and feelings.

Prior to coming to this Guiding Principle, if I felt I was right and the other person was wrong, I became closed to what others felt. Often I'd go into my "You can't stop me if I think I'm right!" act, declaring that what I felt was true and unarguable and I was going to act on it no matter what.

I mentioned that the false payoffs of our acts are that they allow us to be right and make others wrong; either to dominate others or to avoid being dominated. Your acts cost you self-expression, satisfaction, vitality, and well-being, and they keep you out of attunement with yourself and others. The Guiding Principle that *feelings are not facts* reminds me that, no matter how intensely I feel I'm right about something, it's only my feeling. It guides me to realize that being open to other people's feelings, rather than trying to make other people wrong, dominate them, or avoid being dominated by them, gives me the possibility of creating mutually fulfilling relationships.

You can't argue with another person's perceptions.

This Guiding Principle is closely related to "feelings aren't facts." *You can't argue with another person's perceptions* guides and reminds me that we're all individuals. Each person has his or her own perceptions designed by that individual's survival programming, with its unique interpretations. Those interpretations are the stories that he or she made up and that shape that person's unique perceptions, just as the stories in my programming shape mine.

When my perception of a situation differs from someone else's, my Guiding Principle about not being able to argue with another person's perceptions helps me to realize that instead of attempting to invalidate the other person's perception, I need to respect it and discuss our different perceptions with the goal of learning to be attuned to each other. This is part of creating mutually fulfilling relationships.

Conflicting feelings can coexist peacefully until they are coupled with actions.

This Guiding Principle reminds me how to behave appropriately when I find myself in disagreement with another person. The fact that my feelings about something are in conflict with those of another person won't lead to war as long as we don't act out this conflict of feelings. We can express our feelings, but if we start verbally attacking each other, trying to dominate each other, or, on the other hand, withholding ourselves to punish each other for having feelings that conflict with the other person's, we'll create a state of war that can damage the relationship.

Every time something new happens, I go back to my old ways.

This Guiding Principle reminds me that when I experience a situation in the present that my mind interprets as similar to a past situation, my amygdala will generally kidnap my common sense and cue me with my old default programming.

Remembering that *every time something new happens, I go back to my old ways* is vital information. It reminds me that, despite what I've learned through mindful awareness, my old hard-wiring will tend to make me want to go back to my habitual mindless acts. It reminds me that the only way to stop letting my hardwiring run me on automatic is to be mindful: This means interrupting my machinery; dis-identifying with the voice in my head; disengaging from my old Organizing Principles and the acts they trigger; and focusing on my Guiding Principles so that I can be in the present and respond mindfully.

Don't do unto others what you wouldn't have them do unto you.

This Guiding Principle is the original Golden Rule as stated in the Talmud, and learning it has made a tremendous difference in my life.

As a child, I was taught that the Golden Rule was "Do unto others as you would have them do unto you." I interpreted this to mean that I should do everything that other people—especially people close to me—wanted me to do for them. This created pressure for me to do what they wanted, or what I anticipated they wanted. Often I did what others asked of me, even if I didn't want to do it and even if I felt that it wasn't right. In the instances when I didn't do as others wished, I felt guilty and beat myself up for not doing it because I didn't feel that I had the right to have refused. The original Golden Rule from the Talmud, however—*don't do unto others what you wouldn't have them do unto you*—reminds me simply not to harm others. This has enlightened me and "lightened" my life considerably by lifting off my shoulders the obligation I used to feel to please people, regardless of my own feelings.

Don't live with familiar pain out of fear of awkward pain.

This Guiding Principle reminds me that it's self-defeating to stay in a bad situation, repeating old painful behavior patterns just because I'm afraid of what might happen if I leave it and start anew. It reminds me not to stay in my personal prison just because of fear of change! It reminds me that I *can* commit to new behavior that can lead me toward a more fulfilling experience, even though it means I'll have to risk the unfamiliar pain of changing and doing something different.

One way of describing the underlying fear of taking this risk is "You know what you've got but you don't know what you will get!" Often the fear of going from what you've got to something new and not knowing what it will be plays out in keeping you trapped in a bad situation, because you're afraid that as bad as what you've got is, what you will get as its replacement may be worse!

Many of us are afraid of the unknown, but we don't have to allow that fear to keep us trapped in dysfunctional ways of thinking and acting just because we're used to the pain they cause and feel we can tolerate it, however miserably. This Guiding Principle reminds me that the fear of awkward pain is going to be there, but if I want to grow, I have to move ahead despite the fear. It's the only way to open the door to possibility.

Remember this rule: In a situation in which you are in pain and feel that you are in a bind that will keep you there, you have three options from which to choose that will resolve the problem and change your experience. I think of these options as three doors.

You can choose Door 1 and accept the situation fully.

You can choose Door 2 and change the situation.

You can choose Door 3 and remove yourself from the situation.

Choosing any of these options will end the bind that you have been in that has kept you in pain. The point is to not maintain a painful status quo just because you're afraid that choosing Door 1, Door 2, or Door 3 means doing something that you have never done before and, in so doing, you may experience pain.

We can put our bad feelings into others just as they can put theirs into us.

This Guiding Principle reminds me that people often dump their problems onto one another. It reminds me to not allow other people to put their bad feelings into me so that I'm stuck with them.

I first learned this lesson years ago when one of my children received a punishment of not being included in a family vacation. While on vacation, I received a call from her, and at the end of the call she felt fine and I was miserable in the paradise of Hawaii. She shamed and blamed me for punishing her with the net effect that she felt better and I felt worse!

The Guiding Principle *we can put our bad feelings into others just as they can put theirs into us* also reminds me not to dump my bad feelings into other people just because I'm feeling bad and want to relieve myself of those bad feelings. It reminds me that when my machinery takes the driver's seat and I give my bad feelings to others or I accept their bad feelings into me, I'm acting unconsciously. This Guiding Principle keeps me mindful so that I won't allow this to happen.

Life is lived in the little things.

This Guiding Principle reminds me that it's the small events in my daily life—holding hands with my loved ones, visiting with my grandson or talking with him on the phone—that are the most important, and it reminds me to take time to cherish them.

Years ago I read a book that was a collection of "deathbed interviews" in which the author-editor pointed out that terminal patients rarely talked about large business or personal triumphs or failures; rather, they spoke of the little things that brought them happiness. I've seen this in my own life as well. Over the years, when my grown-up children remind me of meaningful moments from their childhoods, they mostly talk about small things like our riding a bike together and rarely mention the material things I gave them. *Life is lived in the little things.*

PAUSE YOUR MACHINERY

- Review your list of Organizing Principles. Identify and write down any beliefs you've been holding that you feel are dysfunctional, and write them down. (Since all of your Organizing Principles may be dysfunctional, this list may be the same as your original list, which you created in Chapter 8.)

- Referring to your list of dysfunctional Organizing Principles, create a new corresponding Guiding Principle to counteract each one. These Guiding Principles will help you to act in healthier ways and support you in remodeling your brain and achieving your goals for self-transformation. For example, if one of your Organizing Principles has been "There's no point in setting goals for myself because I can't achieve them," you might create the new Guiding Principle "I can create and achieve goals for myself because the world is filled with possibility."

One of the goals all of us have is to experience more joy in our lives than pain, yet some of us find ourselves continuing to be unhappy in a relationship or creating pain for ourselves by acting dysfunctionally in situation after situation. Why and how do we do this? And what can we do to break these long-term patterns? That is the subject of the next part of the book.

Part III

FROG IN HOT WATER:

LONG-TERM PATTERNS

THAT CREATE FRUSTRATION

AND SUFFERING AND HOW

TO BREAK THEM

CHAPTER TWELVE

HOW DO YOU BECOME A FROG IN HOT WATER?

I once heard that if you put a frog in a pan of water, put the pan on the stove, and gradually turn up the heat under the pan, the frog would acclimate to the warm water, continue to get used to it as the water becomes increasingly hot, and would remain in the pan until the scalding hot water kills the frog. I later learned that this is apocryphal; in reality, when the water gets hot enough for a frog to feel it, the frog will jump out. The difference between frogs and people is that often we just remain in hot water as it continues heating up, even though we are distressed by the rising temperature.

I define "frog-in-hot-water" experiences as those situations and relationships that become less and less satisfying and increasingly painful to us over long periods, either because we stay in the same painful situation or engage in serial situations and relationships in which we have the same kind of painful experience.

Frog-in-hot-water relationships can persist for years, and as such they become the epitome of the dysfunctional patterns of behavior we've discussed. They are also very common.

Every day the media tell us about new frog-in-hot-water situations: politicians who repeatedly have sexual affairs at the cost of their reputations and the humiliation their actions bring to themselves and their families; celebrities who go from one bad marriage or one self-destructive situation to another.

And every day I see frog-in-hot-water situations in the lives of people I know. Here is a brief sampling.

- A friend of mine has a daughter who's been in a troubled relationship for ten years. She wants to marry and her boyfriend never commits. Not a day goes by in which my friend's daughter isn't miserable, yet she's devoted to her boyfriend and is always hoping it will work out.
- I know two widowed sisters—one sister is eighty, the other eighty-five—who live together and have been fighting with each other since childhood in an unending mud fight.
- Another friend, who's now in his forties, has been fighting since he was a teenager with his father, looking and waiting for acknowledgment and respect and never receiving it.

I became fascinated with frog-in-hot-water experiences a few years ago when I was doing research for this book. I reread the thirty-three years of entries I'd written in my journal and was shocked to see that I had said the same things in 1983, when I'd been married for five years and started to keep my journal, as I did in 2005 about the frustrations that eventually caused the end of my marriage after twenty-seven years.

I was amazed to realize that I was in pain when I made those first journal entries and that the pain only got worse year after year. My wife and I were both "frogs in boiling water"; why, for all that time, which included hundreds of therapy sessions, didn't the two of us make peace with the situation, fix it, or leave it?

In this section of the book, I'm going to apply what I've discussed about the mind and the brain to explain why and how some of us remain frogs who sit suffering in our pans of hot water, and how, if you're in this type of situation, you can learn to make the choice to turn off the heat or jump out of the pan.

Earlier I said that there are always three ways to end your suffering in any circumstance in which you're in pain: Door 1—accept the situation exactly as it is, warts and all; Door 2—change the situation; or Door 3—remove yourself from the situation. So, it may seem as if the answer is simple: If you're in a pan of hot water, just choose one of these doors and you'll no longer be a frog suffering in hot water.

Although the solution of choosing one of the three doors is simple, *actually choosing a door* is extremely challenging for some of us, at least in certain circumstances. Looking at how and why we remain a frog in hot water is only the first step; the second step is learning what we must do to choose a door; the third, and perhaps hardest, step is having the resolve to do what's necessary to continually interrupt our machinery's default system that's keeping us stuck, so that we can make a mindful choice to accept the situation, change it, or leave it. Part of this is having the resolve to stick to our choice even if we believe that, painful as it is, we can survive the pain of our frog-in-hot-water situation and we fear the unknown awkward pain of change.

I'm sharing my experience because I think it's typical of the patterns that keep so many of us stuck.

I was first married at twenty-two. In hindsight, I realize that at the time of my marriage I was immature, totally unaware that I wasn't the voice in my head and that I had no conception of the here and now. I believed that my feelings were facts and I acted accordingly. I wasn't reading the music of my own life; instead, I was doing what I believed I was supposed to do, based on what my contemporaries were doing, and what I believed was right according to custom. I was a player piano, and each new event determined which old piece of music would be replayed on my machinery's dysfunctional programming. I hadn't come to understand mindfulness or being able to observe what was going on within myself and in my relationships. Put simply, I was almost 100 percent not present; I hadn't any inkling that my machinery and its default programming were running my life.

I left my first marriage at thirty-one. I spent the next five years in therapy, self-actualization workshops, and studying the latest and greatest books about consciousness. My machinery and programming were well on their way to a "home makeover" consisting of concepts I'd learned intellectually about what was causing me to act and think as I did. I'd strengthened my self-esteem through professional achievements. My financial success had gone from "kid-sized" to "man-sized" success. By my mid-thirties, I was confident about myself and knew how to "operate"' with a much improved sense of self-esteem. That, coupled with my inner world's growth, made me feel that I was ready for my second marriage. I remarried at thirty-six and believed we would have a loving, harmonious, and joyous marriage.

With 20/20 hindsight, I now see that I was still dragging around some of my old dysfunctional programming without a clue about how it would impact my second marriage.

As you know, our neural networks are constantly sending signals to and receiving signals from each other. I see this as a kind of Wi-Fi system that is always in search of other people with similar wiring systems. This was the case with my second wife and me. We were drawn together by similar experiences in our early lives. My wife's father, whom she had loved, had died when she was just a little older than I'd been when my father had died, and both of our mothers were of the "wire monkey" school, which gave us a strong common bond.

How a Myth about Yourself Can Keep You in Hot Water

In hindsight, I see that I brought a myth into the marriage. The myth was that I, and I alone, was a "recovering" emotionally challenged person, constantly needing adjustment and repair, and that when it came to relationships, I couldn't trust myself. I also had a belief that my wife was the opposite.

I recognize now that the myth was just another outgrowth of my "Poor me" act, justifying my feeling broken and enabling me to remain broken in my own mind and maybe in my wife's thinking. In reality, I wasn't doomed to be broken; I just wasn't yet able to heal and transform myself. But at the time, of course, I didn't see this, and I didn't see "I am the broken one" as a myth; I saw it as a *fact* instead of a *feeling*!

This myth is important because it's one of the factors that held me captive as a frog in hot water.

When we're stuck in frog-in-hot-water situations or relationships, I believe that one or more myths like mine are always contributing to keeping us in the pan while the water continues heating up.

My second wife, like my first wife, is a lovely person inside and out. Anything I'm writing about is purely from my perspective because it's the only perspective about which I can speak with authority.

Our marriage had all the traditional flashpoints for arguments: money, sex, and family issues. Although I didn't realize it during our marriage, all of the persistent, unresolved frustrations that came from these issues, and the activation and pain that resulted from them, were really our respective machinery being at war with each other.

During the marriage, one of my machinery's mantras was "I'm doing the right thing for the right reasons, so eventually it'll work out. It only takes patience." But this was just magical thinking on my part, and the magical thinking kept me going for years because, despite the pain I knew I was in, and despite doing the same things over and over again, I kept telling myself that "eventually it'll work out."

Today I can mindfully ask myself why we endured arguing for so long and neither of us ever chose to fully accept, change, or leave the situation. The answer I can give for myself is that even though at times I was mindful and realized that the only way I could change my experience was to choose Door 1, 2, or 3, I didn't support that insight with the resolve to act on it. When we couple mindfulness with resolve, we can create new behavior. But without the resolve, we can't take advantage of our brain's neuroplasticity and create the new neural pathways needed to create new behavior.

Insight can be fleeting, and without the combination of mindfulness and resolve to *act* on your insight, your machinery will run and own you instead of you running and owning your machinery. Without the resolve to act mindfully, you will go back to operating on automatic pilot, reinforcing your old neural networks that support you doing the same things again and again instead of creating new neural networks that will support healthier behavior. But as we've discussed and will continue to explore, *you can develop this resolve.*

PAUSE YOUR MACHINERY

- Think mindfully about whether you're currently in a frog-in-hot-water relationship (with your significant other, mother, father, or other family member, or friend) or a frog-in-hot-water situation (such as a job). Do you see the potential for a relationship or situation to become a frog-in-hot-water experience? If so, describe in writing what elements of the relationship or situation are persistently causing you pain or have the potential to do so. Also describe how long you have been experiencing these problems.

- If you're in a frog-in-hot-water relationship or situation, describe the reasons you are staying there and what is preventing you from choosing Door 1, 2, or 3.

- If you're in a relationship or situation that could potentially become a frog-in-hot-water one, write down the factors that you recognize as determining qualities. What signals tell you to stay? Which ones tell you to change? Describe your role in having created the relationship or the situation as it is right this minute. Then define the role you see for yourself in the future in influencing it either to become a frog-in-hot-water relationship or situation or to avoid becoming one.

As long as my lack of resolve kept allowing my machinery to run me, I couldn't choose Door 1, 2, or 3; I couldn't resolve the arguments or end my pain. Why did I lack the resolve to change? And how did I eventually develop it? I'll answer these two vital questions in the following chapters, but let's first look at the process by which we can allow our machinery to make us frogs in hot water, even when we desperately want to stop being in pain.

CHAPTER THIRTEEN

RECOGNIZING YOUR RESISTANCE TO CHANGE—AND WHAT YOU CAN DO ABOUT IT

..... 🧠 .....

When we act like a frog in a pan of hot water, it's because our default programming is controlling our actions. Our machinery—at the level of our neural pathways—just keeps doing what it has done before. Indeed, it is programmed *not* to change, because along with the early experiences, interpretations, and judgments embedded in our machinery's programming, our programming also contains defense mechanisms that protect these beliefs about ourselves and the world by justifying, dismissing, or attacking any outside input that might lead to change. It's generally a struggle for new ideas—bottom-up information—to get through because our defense mechanisms tend to give our brain a bias toward top-down processing that blocks the new information by stonewalling it.

But this doesn't mean you can't change. What it means is that as long as you're on automatic pilot you will continue to use your past-based strategies even if they haven't worked and even if they're useless and destructive. By allowing this to continue, you will keep doing the same things, or variations of them, for your whole life, even if they don't work.

So if you're a frog in hot water, in order to act in a new way and create the possibility of a new and more fulfilling experience—that is, in order to stop being in hotter and hotter water—you will have to use the brain's remarkable capacity for being reshaped. This takes intention and it takes a commitment of your will. And of course it takes mindfulness.

Simply put, mindfulness and the resolve to continue being mindful help us overcome our machinery's resistance and to change our lives. Every mindful act reinforces our new behavior as the brain's malleability allows us to create new neural pathways for healthier living. The more often we act mindfully, the more often our new neural pathways will be the pathways along which our neurons fire.

This is how a change that initially is temporary can become a permanent trait. When you make a change like this, your brain is still functioning the same way; in other words, it is still firing neurons along neural pathways. But because you are developing new neural pathways through mindfulness, your brain starts firing neurons along the new neural pathways, which gradually become developed to a great enough extent that your old neural pathways don't have as much habitual "pull" as they previously did.

My old Organizing Principles—primarily those having to do with fear of abandonment, control, painful feelings, and trust—kept me in a painful bind in my marriage for years, like the frog in the pan of increasingly hot water, and also for years in my relationships with my children and my business partner. I kept choosing familiar pain over the unknown because of my attachments to these people. I couldn't believe the issues wouldn't somehow be resolved, that the relationships wouldn't become harmonious.

My default programming kept me from consistently asking for what I wanted in these relationships. I would ask for what I wanted for a while, or I would put out a trial balloon to see how the other person would react to my requests. But if I sensed that the answer was going to be "No," then I'd back off because my default programming made me so afraid that if I committed to a stance to get what I wanted, they would abandon me, creating pain I couldn't bear.

What's Wrong with Being Right?

In these relationships, my default programming also directed a lot of my thoughts and feelings in support of my being "right." Sometimes the desire to be right makes us attempt to make the other person wrong; sometimes it makes us withdraw into ourselves, as I did when I'd back off from taking a stance to get my needs met. Withdrawing into ourselves can allow us to feel that we're "right" inside, even though we're not getting what we want, because internally we can judge the other person as wrong for not giving us what we want.

Now I know what I didn't know then: The desire to be "right" is always the objective of your machinery and programming, not of your being. Your being doesn't need to be right; to your being, there is no right and there is no wrong. To your being, there is just what is. Right and wrong are judgments and interpretations, and they come from your past and keep you in the past. When you are mindful and dissolve the judgments and interpretations that arise in your mind, you are left with just what is.

When you recognize what is as simply being what it is, you create the possibility of resolving conflicts because you're in the present instead of reacting from your machinery. This creates possibility for change because you're not being held captive to your past and to repeating past behavior.

Letting Your Negative Expectations Control You Keeps You in Hot Water

When we're on automatic pilot, we see what we expect to see and hear what we expect to hear, but we don't recognize this. We believe that we are actually hearing and seeing accurately and we react accordingly. I've found that we assign more weight to what we expect than to its opposite: If someone says what we don't expect to hear, we tend to forget it quickly, whereas we remember forever what we think we heard that matched our expectations. I kept expecting people close to me to shame and blame me, so even if they didn't, often I still heard their words as if they did and, without necessarily realizing it, I automatically and quickly dismissed whatever they might have said that was the opposite.

Subscribing to the myth that I was "the broken one" kept me in a closed circle of having the same experiences again and again. I had no idea this was a myth or what this myth cost me, no idea that it was part of my defenses that were keeping me from growing and from being happier. I was unaware that I was letting my machinery run me. I wanted sympathy, I wanted understanding, and I felt that

I deserved them because I was broken. Believing this myth myself, I didn't know that I could heal and change.

I hadn't yet created new Guiding Principles that would empower me to act in ways that would be healthy and productive rather than self-defeating. Mindfulness was still mostly a concept to me rather than a way of life that I consistently practiced. I didn't yet see that all the understanding I had of my programming didn't mean a thing if I didn't continually interrupt my machinery and make mindful choices. The tug of my machinery and default programming on my mind and body, the anxiety and the fear it created in me, was so strong that I needed to be far clearer about it than I was. I needed the resolve within myself to be able to change.

The potential resolve was within me, and the ability to be mindful was already intermittently there, but until, as I'll discuss later, I finally experienced such intense pain from the situation that I couldn't bear it, I allowed the pull of my machinery and default programming to keep sweeping me out to sea as the undertow in the ocean can sweep an unwary swimmer farther and farther from shore.

Had I been in the present, I could have mindfully seen that I wasn't my "poor me" act or my "broken one" myth. I was a man who had accomplished a lot and worked hard to learn life lessons that I could apply effectively *if I used the power of mindfulness—* which all of us have—*and backed it up with the resolve to change.* But I wasn't there yet.

I discovered that one of the consequences of my inability to accept and express my own anger was that, without knowing it, I'd make others around me angry so that, in effect, they would be expressing my anger for me. This unconscious round-robin of anger would occur when I'd do things that I should have known would upset those close to me. How much more effective it would have been if I'd been able to consciously acknowledge and express my own anger. If I'd been able to, it might even have helped me find a better way to resolve the problems.

My myth of being "the broken one" was destructive for me in terms of my personal growth. The myth declared that if there was a problem, it was totally my responsibility because I was "the broken one." This is clear to me now, but as long as I still permitted my programming to run me, I was doomed to act in the same dysfunctional ways, continually recommitting to my role as being broken. I wasn't willing to face the awkward pain of changing, so I remained a frog in hot water!

PAUSE YOUR MACHINERY

Consider the following questions and write your answers in your notebook or computer file:

- Do you repeatedly have fights about the same issue or issues with your significant other, a family member, a friend, or someone you work with? Describe the issue. Think mindfully to see if unconsciously you may be investing the issue with another meaning. For example, if you're continually fighting with your significant other about his being what you consider messy in your home, and he ignores your requests to be neater and gets defensive, are you interpreting this as a lack of respect for you?

Are you further interpreting the lack of respect as a lack of loving you? Describe any meanings that you now recognize as being the underlying issue(s) about which you've been fighting.

- Think mindfully about whether your programming is causing you to overreact in these fights. (Sometimes a lack of neatness is just a lack of neatness in the other person's habits; it doesn't necessarily have to do with his or her feelings about you.)

  ○ If you conclude that you're taking something personally that isn't really personal, you can resolve the issue within yourself. If you feel that you need to address the underlying issue mindfully with the other person, have a conversation about the real issue, not the "cover" issue.

  ○ If you and your partner are continually fighting about money, are you really fighting about money or are you really fighting about control? Are one or both of you, perhaps unconsciously, trying to use money to control the other or reacting because you feel the other person is trying to control you? Or is money a cover issue for fighting about love? Do one or both of you feel that if your partner doesn't agree with your perspective about spending money, the other person doesn't love you?

- Remember that when you are mindful, you are not defensive; you are in the present, you are open to possibility, to authentic communication; you're not coming in with a preconceived notion of "right" and "wrong" to which you're going to pressure the other person to acquiesce. That's not being mindful; it's being run by your machinery!

- If you're in a frog-in-hot-water relationship or situation or one that has the potential to become one, think mindfully about whether you may have been acting on automatic pilot in ways that are causing problems in your relationship or situation. For example, do you sometimes act on automatic pilot and behave impulsively when it would be better for you to think before you act? Or, if your default programming judges anger to be "wrong" or "bad," do you suppress your anger and act in a passive or passive-aggressive way that causes other people to be angry at you? Do you act angrily without recognizing it or taking responsibility for it?

- Fear is also an important emotion to look at in terms of a frog-in-hot-water relationship or situation. What fears are embedded in your programming and how do they affect this relationship or situation?

- Describe any other dysfunctional elements in your programming that, when you're on automatic pilot, are resulting in your behaving in ways that encourage the persistence of your frog-in-hot-water relationship or situation.

- In a frog-in-hot-water relationship or situation or one that has the potential to become one, do you feel shamed or blamed by another person's comments that are critical of the way you act? If so, describe the comments. Do your best to write them accurately, using the words that the person actually spoke.

- When you've finished, think mindfully about whether in reality the person was shaming or blaming you or if it was your listening that made you interpret these comments this way because of your own inner critic.

- ○ If you conclude that the person wasn't shaming or blaming you but rather you reacted from your programming, it opens the space for you to hear and consider the other person's feedback in a new way that allows for possibility.
- ○ If you conclude that the person was actually shaming or blaming you, have a conversation with the other person about how you feel when this happens. Explain how he or she can express herself or himself to you in such a way that you won't be hurt or defensive and can instead hear the feedback and be open to modifying your behavior.
- Did you bring a myth with you into the relationship or situation? If so, describe this myth. For example, you might have brought in the myth that you are a savior who will cure everything that's wrong with the other person or that he or she will cure everything that's wrong with you and solve all your problems.
- If you did bring in a myth, describe how you came to believe this myth about yourself. What would it take for you to release the myth and live free of its obligations and restrictions?

In the next chapter, we'll look more closely at other ways that our default programming can make us vulnerable to being frogs in hot water. We'll also look at how we can learn to recognize this, the first step to disengaging from it.

CHAPTER FOURTEEN

A FIRST STEP TOWARD CHOOSING A DOOR: ANALYZING THE BIND THAT KEEPS YOU A FROG IN HOT WATER

..... 🧠 .....

You have to be in a bind to be a frog in hot water: You feel that, for one reason or another, it's impossible to end your suffering by accepting your situation, changing it, or removing yourself from it. It feels as if there are no other options but to remain where you are, so you feel powerless and a victim—of another person, circumstances, the world, or life.

The primary feeling that kept me in a bind was the fear both of being alone and of hurting myself and others emotionally. I hadn't yet learned the vital lesson that with mindfulness and resolve I could override the fear that the amygdala, because of my programming, was sending into my system; that by continuing to practice mindfulness and resolve I could act despite the fear, and in time, I could actually unlearn the fear.

Although it's clear that my programming's avoidance techniques are self-defeating, when my machinery and programming are running me on automatic pilot, I don't see the consequences clearly. Even if I glimpse them, if I remain on automatic pilot I allow my dysfunctional programming to run me. Remember, all our machinery and programming can do on automatic pilot is to do what they've always done. In so doing, they reinforce the pattern of working the way they've always worked, firing the same neurons along the same neural pathways, regardless of the results. When we're on automatic pilot, the brain will do what is familiar, even if it's useless or destructive!

By allowing my fear of abandonment to put me in a bind instead of overriding it with mindful awareness, I continued to be run by my programming's strategies for backing away from my real thoughts and feelings, even about the most significant issues in my life affecting my marriage and other frog-in-hot-water relationships, and even though the water was getting hotter and hotter.

During my marriage, consciously I wanted to be happy, so it's natural to wonder how I could have allowed myself to let my default programming run me in ways that kept me unhappy. The two major ways that my mind on automatic pilot supported my staying a frog in hot water were denial and rationalization.

I'd experienced so much pain in childhood that I developed a denial mechanism I refer to as "an amnesia for pain." When my unhappiness would become so painful I couldn't deny it, my default programming rationalized it with the belief that suffering was just part of life and I shouldn't expect anything else. This is an example of the internal feeling of being "right" that our default programming can give us to justify our being unhappy and to block the idea that there's something we can do about it.

The reality was that if I'd been mindful and acknowledged to myself that I was the one putting myself in a bind with the disempowering belief that suffering was just part of life and there was nothing I could do about it, I could have taken action to do something about it. If I'd done this, my life would have been happier, and the other people in relationships with me—my wife, my children, my business partner—would have also benefited from it. A large part of the reason I didn't acknowledge this to myself can be summed up in one word: fear.

Overcoming Fear of Awkward Pain

I mentioned that one of the new Guiding Principles I've created to help me act in ways that are healthier and more productive is "Don't live with familiar pain out of fear of awkward pain." Fear of awkward pain is an outgrowth of fear of the unknown, and, by definition, change is the unknown. My default programming told me that if I committed to the stance of getting my needs met in my marriage and other frog-in-hot-water relationships, I would be abandoned and I might not survive the awkward, unknown pain I would experience, so it was better to live with the familiar pain than to take a stand for change.

There is an irony in this. In the day-to-day negotiations for my business, I'm not, and never have been, afraid to take a stance or make a demand. Historically I've always been an effective and strong negotiator who frequently gets what I ask for or am able to negotiate a mutually satisfactory agreement. If a negotiation doesn't work out, I walk away with no regrets. The contrast between the part of me that easily and unequivocally stands up for myself in business deals and the part that wavered in my closest loving relationships underlines the power that I allowed my fear to have over my behavior in the relationships that mean a great deal to me.

My amnesia for pain kept me from experiencing it profoundly enough for it to move me to commit to taking a stance for change. Rationalizing the pain when I did feel it, by justifying it with the cynical view that life is always painful, kept me in the past instead of the present and removed the possibility of change.

It's a true challenge to be mindfully aware 100 percent of the time, but it's easy to be in your machinery 100 percent of the time. Instead of being mindful and creating new and more productive behavior by creating new neural pathways in your brain, you can let the same neurons fire along the same neural pathways and reproduce the same behavior with the same results year after year after year. You can be a frog in hot water and feel like a victim of somebody else (or the world or just life) when the only thing you're really a victim of is your own default programming running you on automatic pilot instead of your using your ability to couple mindfulness with resolve and choose Door 1, 2, or 3. I created the Guiding Principle "Don't live with familiar pain out of fear of awkward pain" when, after I stopped being a frog in hot water, I saw how heavily my fear of awkward pain had contributed to my remaining one for so long.

·········· PAUSE YOUR MACHINERY ··········

- Think about the relationship or situation you've identified as a frog-in-hot-water experience or as having the potential to become one. Describe in writing the bind that is keeping you there instead of choosing Door 1, 2, or 3. (Refer to your answers from the exercise at the end of Chapter 12 describing your reasons for staying in the situation and see if it helps you to describe the bind.)

- Describe the beliefs that are keeping you in the bind. Describe whether any of these beliefs are in conflict with each other. Describe any beliefs you have about life, fate, yourself, and the world that contribute to your rationalizing the bind you're in instead of acting to end it.

- If you brought a myth into the relationship or situation, describe how the myth serves your default programming, and how it contributes to keeping you in the bind. Include in this a description of how the myth prevents you from seeing yourself in a fuller way.

- Describe the feelings, such as fear, that are keeping you in the bind instead of acting to end it. And remember that just as there are plenty of frogs in hot water there are also a lot of other fish in the sea!

Other factors in our default programming can also contribute to our remaining a frog in hot water. In the next chapter, I'll share with you the ones that were most powerful in keeping me there for so long.

CHAPTER FIFTEEN

OTHER WAYS THAT YOU CAN KEEP YOURSELF STUCK

····· 🧠 ·····

Regardless of how rational and objective we tell ourselves we're being, when we are on automatic pilot we are in the service of our machinery; consequently, we're generally not accurately seeing whatever circumstance we're in. This is what makes denial and rationalization possible. And our machinery is always ready to kidnap our common sense via intellectualizations that create the binds that caused the frog-in-hot-water experience to happen.

During the time when you're allowing your machinery to run you, your conscious mind is filled with a muddle of your old beliefs. You see these old beliefs as truths instead of opinions. And because they are often dysfunctional and in conflict with each other, they not only put you in a bind, they keep you there. When you're on automatic pilot, these beliefs become your operating manual for your default behavior, determining your every action and reaction.

In the previous chapter, I mentioned that I rationalized suffering in my marriage and other close relationships with the self-defeating belief that life was full of suffering and there was nothing I could do about it. For many years (as I described in Chapter 8), my Organizing Principles made it impossible for me to act effectively to accomplish my conscious goals of harmony in my family relationships and in my relationship with my business partner. These Organizing Principles were so key to my remaining a frog in hot water that I'm going to review a few of them here to further illustrate how dysfunctional beliefs keep us in painful situations.

My Organizing Principle "Painful feelings are dangerous (and all feelings have the potential to be painful, so all feelings are dangerous)" continually reinforced my amnesia for pain. When you repress your pain as well as your other feelings, as I did, it keeps raising the threshold of the pain you'll tolerate. Part of what created the pain I experienced was the fact that my Organizing Principle "Eventually, loving others will make things work out" was in conflict with my other principles "The world isn't safe; don't trust," "No one will take care of my needs but me," and "If they really loved me, they'd never put me in an uncomfortable position." I couldn't really love anyone if I felt that I couldn't trust them and they couldn't take care of my needs, and that if they really loved me they would never ask me for something that makes me uncomfortable.

As long as I let these beliefs run me, they put me in a bind through which I stayed a frog in hot water. And, as long as I allowed myself to continue running on automatic pilot, I didn't recognize that I was the one responsible for creating and holding on to these beliefs and that, in fact, I had an alternative: I could mindfully let go of them.

It's important to remember that the reason the dysfunctional beliefs embedded in our programming can make us frogs in hot water is they govern both how we view our situation and how we act. So do our fears. As you know, one of the old beliefs embedded in my programming was that I couldn't trust other people; various fears from my early experiences were also embedded in my programming. Eventually I recognized how these two factors affected my behavior in a very specific way that contributed to my becoming and remaining a frog in hot water.

Saving a Crust of Bread

Connie Weisman, one of my first spiritual guides, told a story that profoundly illustrates how fear and mistrust prevent people from truly sharing all they have to share, even though there is no logical reason for withholding and doing so is self-destructive.

Two Russian political prisoners in the 1970s became incredibly close friends in a Siberian prison camp. The prison had no walls because the frigid climate, the ever-present snow, and the long distance to the closest village prevented prisoners from attempting an escape. After many years, the two men agreed they would rather die than continue their present existence, so they decided to escape—or die trying.

They started saving crusts of bread to sustain them on their journey to freedom. When they had enough bread crusts, they started out. The journey was even more difficult than they had anticipated. Finally they ran out of food and neither of them could go a step further. They collapsed in the snow, prepared to die, not knowing that a village and safety were only a hundred yards away. When the villagers found the two escapees, they were unconscious and close to death. Back in the village, where the men were being revived in hospital beds, the villagers found that each man had one crust of bread hidden in his tattered clothing—a crust of bread that he had withheld from the other and had been saving for himself alone. Even at the end, as they were about to collapse and probably die, neither man took that crust of bread from his pocket to share with his friend.

In hindsight, I now see that because of my fears I withheld a part of me, even in my marriage. That was my emotional crust of bread. Without being aware of it, I was experiencing life within the prison of my own default programming!

I longed for the feeling of unconditional love and safety, but since I'd never experienced it in my childhood, I didn't know how to create it or why I didn't have it. Now I understand how critical our early attachments are to our future relationships.

How Your Early Attachments Shape Your Relationships Until You Start Changing Your Wiring

I can't emphasize enough how the type of attachment bond you start out with impacts your relationships. When your needs for affirmation and affection are not met in childhood, you settle into a pattern of expecting that your needs will never be met, and this makes it even harder to have your needs met. If, as a child, you haven't experienced the sense of safety and love that you need from your parents, then you don't have a sense of what it is. As a result, you feel emotionally disconnected from your parents, and when you become an adult, you bring those same painful needs for attachment into your romantic relationships. Yet because you've never experienced that sense of connection, and although you long for it, you don't really know it exists nor do you know how to provide it for others.

Discussing pioneering psychologist John Bowlby's contributions to the study of attachment theory and attachment behaviors, Jeffrey M. Lance, Ph.D., wrote that Bowlby believed such behaviors to actually be "built in, innate psychobiological needs [that is to say] we have to attach no matter how bad the early connections are, and we will carry the particular form and struggles of these early attachments into our adult lives, . . . [including the] unmet longings, fears, and protective strategies [which resulted] from these connections."[1] This view is supported by Diane Ackerman's reporting, mentioned earlier, of research showing that the imprints from our attachments in infancy start patterns of thinking, behavior, self-image, and choices about intimate relationships that we bring with us into adulthood.[2] But, as we know from Andrew Curran, Daniel Siegel, and Richard Davidson, the neuroplasticity of our brains makes it possible for us to change and create more satisfying intimate relationships than we were capable of creating when we started out.

One of the things that make it challenging to work our way from an attachment in childhood that wasn't secure to learning how to have a secure, loving attachment as an adult is the importance of the parent-child attachment in developing the seven executive functions that I discussed in Chapter 9: regulating your body, attuned communication, emotional balance, response flexibility, insight, empathy, and modulating fear. All of these are compromised when your childhood attachment isn't secure. The degree to which these abilities are developed or not developed influences our self-image; our mental, emotional, and physical health; our ability to tune in to ourselves and to others; and our capacity to act in productive ways and, thus, to interact with others.

This information explains why, if you haven't had a secure attachment with your parents in childhood, you may have the tendency to re-create that unsatisfying and potentially self-defeating relationship as an adult. All of these factors manifested in me as my amnesia for pain, my unconscious silently dominating me with fears, my internal critic always siding with the other person, and as a lack of attunement to myself and to others. These are all consequences of the absence of security I experienced in childhood, my earliest experience of attachment.

As much as I craved deep closeness, unconsciously I also feared it. The most famous line from Tennyson's poem "In Memoriam" is "'Tis better to have loved and lost/than never to have loved at all." I believe that after losing my father and experiencing my mother's unavailability, I was so afraid of really loving and then losing someone that unconsciously, in my marriage as well as in other close relationships, it caused me to withhold part of myself. I perceived the pain of loss as so devastating that I think my unconscious mind didn't believe it could be better to risk loving, and possibly losing that love, than never to love in the first place. Although I was unaware of it at the time, I think that, contrary to Tennyson, the belief in my programming was "'Tis better not to love fully than to risk the pain of losing love."

Reflecting on it today, I recognize that in my marriage especially I needed to take a stand despite my fears. I needed to break the binds in which I'd imprisoned myself by my fears, my beliefs, my identity. I finally tackled the issues that created the binds, and started making mindful choices so that I wouldn't continue to be a frog in hot water. It took years, but I finally did change. By so doing, I learned a great deal that has set me on a new and healthier course for the rest of my life.

PAUSE YOUR MACHINERY

- If you're not choosing Door 1, describe in writing the specific elements of the relationship or situation that make you choose not to accept it warts and all.
- If you're not choosing Door 2, describe why you aren't changing it. Have you committed to changing yourself or do you just want the other person (or persons) to change? If you have changed, is the other person changing or committed to changing?
- If you're not choosing Door 3, describe why you aren't leaving it. What are your emotional reasons? What are your intellectual reasons?
- Referring to your exercise at the end of Chapter 7, think mindfully about whether your identity is preventing you from choosing Door 1, 2, or 3. If so, describe how.
- Do you feel that you have "amnesia for pain"? If so, describe how it works and how, up till now, it has made you a frog in hot water or has the potential to make you a frog in hot water. When you feel pain, describe what happens when the amnesia

for pain starts its process that soon makes you suppress it, forget about it, ignore it, or anesthetize yourself so that you become numb and live with it.

In the next chapter, we'll discuss the process of disengaging from the programming that keeps us in hot water and making a mindful choice to accept the situation, change it, or leave it.

CHAPTER SIXTEEN

CHOOSING A DOOR

..... 🧠 .....

The Law of Inertia is a basic law of physics. It states that an inert object—that is, an object at rest—stays at rest and an object in motion stays in motion unless it is acted upon by an external force.

Since human beings on automatic pilot keep doing the same things again and again, we may look as if we're in motion, but when we allow our machinery and programming to run us, we are actually inert. The only way for us to move toward healthier behavior is for a force to be applied to set us in motion.

Although in certain instances this force can be an external one—a catastrophic event that breaks the hold our machinery may have on us and catalyzes us to act in new ways to survive the crisis—unlike an inert object that requires an external force to move, ultimately the force that creates forward movement in our lives almost always must come from within ourselves. This is the force we create when we begin practicing mindful awareness, making mindful choices, and creating new, healthier ways of thinking and acting instead of responding to everyone and everything from our default programming.

There's a Zen story about three kinds of horses, told from the viewpoint of a jockey who rides all three horses in different races and has to get each mount to put its total energy into its race. The jockey signals the first mount to make its move by merely showing the horse his whip, and the horse gives it his all. With the second horse, the jockey shows the whip, but the horse doesn't respond, and the jockey needs to give it a few whips to get it to really move. The third horse sees the whip and doesn't move, then gets whipped, and still doesn't make its move. In order to move, it needs to be whipped again and again until it feels the jockey's message in the marrow of its bones.

I needed to feel the pain from my marriage in the marrow of my bones before I could find the resolve to alleviate the pain by being mindful instead of allowing my fears, my Organizing Principles, and the rest of my identity to keep me imprisoned in repeating the same old behaviors that had sustained me as a frog in hot water for so many years. It took that critical mass of pain—so much that it totally overcame my amnesia for pain—to make me focus on the fact that through mindful awareness I *could* change, and that it was *up to me* to decide if I wanted to apply the resolve I needed to do so!

At that point I became determined not to let my fears of abandonment and awkward pain own me anymore. I committed to staying mindful and not letting my machinery pull me back into amnesia for pain. My programming was still operating, the voice in my head was still speaking to me as loudly as ever, but my desire to alleviate the pain and to have a more fulfilling relationship was so strong that I kept focusing on the present and using mindfulness to interrupt my machinery.

I considered Door 1 and knew that I did not want to fully accept the relationship my wife and I had as it was. I committed to opening Door 2 to change the relationship with the goal of making it work for both of us. To do this, I knew I had to acknowledge my authentic thoughts and feelings and to express what I wanted and needed. In addition, I had to surrender the part of myself that I'd been withholding in an attempt to be in control and be "safe"; I gave up my last crust of bread.

I finally took a stand for what I wanted and I committed to not backing away. I was in the unknown, and it felt like I was walking on a tightrope without a net. My fears were still roiling in my gut and making me anxious, but when my mindfulness and resolve wavered and I would slip into letting my programming run me, I would focus my mind again in the present so that I could ignore the voice in my head and stay committed to my stand for changing myself so that we would achieve positive change in our marriage.

When, by the following year, the change didn't happen and instead the pain continued to intensify, I moved from Door 2 to Door 3 and left my wife. The decision to get a divorce, and the process of adjusting to the end of our marriage and to my being on my own, was very painful. I survived the awkward pain of being alone that I had feared for so long, gradually accepted the fact that I was on my own, and, over time, began to experience a sense of possibility.

By choosing to no longer be a frog in hot water, I'd finally changed and made choices with mindful awareness. It's crucial to remember that mindfully choosing *any* of the doors—Door 1, accepting the situation fully; Door 2, changing it; or Door 3, leaving it—transforms a frog-in-hot-water situation or relationship into one in which you are no longer suffering. If you're in a frog-in-hot-water situation or relationship, or one that has the potential to be, it's up to you to recognize how much pain you need to feel before you have the resolve to be mindful and choose a door. There is usually a *breakdown* before there is a *breakthrough*.

Will you be like the first kind of horse, which only has to see the whip, and mindfully make a choice about which door you will choose to prevent the situation from causing you long-term pain? Will you be like the second kind of horse and need to feel pain for some time before you summon the resolve to stop yourself from running on automatic, which will just perpetuate your being a frog in hot water in pain, and make a mindful choice about which door to choose? Or will you need to feel pain in the marrow of your bones by letting the situation or relationship persist for a long time before you finally summon the resolve to mindfully dis-identify with and disengage from your old beliefs and behavior? Before you mindfully choose to embrace the situation or relationship by accepting it fully, warts and all, changing it, or leaving it?

Before looking at additional information about preventing or shortening frog-in-hot-water situations and relationships, if you're in such a situation or relationship or one with that potential, please do the following exercise.

PAUSE YOUR MACHINERY

- Describe in writing the kind of horse you are. Is there a kind of horse you would rather be? If so, write down which one.

- Think mindfully about which door you want to choose: 1, 2, or 3. Write down your choice.

- Think mindfully about whether up to this moment the fear of awkward pain is keeping you from choosing a door. If so, describe what you imagine it will be like if you choose the door you want to choose, what kind of pain you believe will follow from the choice, and why you fear that you will be unequipped to cope with it.

- Review what you've just written. Now review what you've written in earlier exercises about the self-judgments, traumas, core issues, fears, and beliefs that have created and are embedded in your programming. Are the fears you have about choosing a door the same as or similar to the fears you identified as being part of your default programming? Do the limitations you described yourself as having that make you afraid you don't have the ability to cope with awkward pain stem from self-judgments that you've identified in earlier exercises as part of your default programming?

- If you recognize that your fear of awkward pain is coming from your default programming, then the solution is to resolve to be mindful so that, instead of continuing to be controlled by the past, you will be in the present, where you can mindfully choose a door that will stop you from being or becoming a frog in hot water.

..... 🧠 .....

In the following chapter, I'll share with you the seven lessons I learned from being a frog in hot water and finally making a choice. I believe they will be helpful to you if you're in either a frog-in-hot-water relationship or situation or one with that potential. If you're not in such a situation, I believe they will help you to avoid getting into one in the future.

CHAPTER SEVENTEEN

SEVEN LESSONS I LEARNED FROM BEING A FROG IN HOT WATER AND FINALLY CHOOSING A DOOR

····· 🧠 ·····

Here are the lessons I've learned from reflecting on being a frog in hot water and on choosing to end the pattern of living on automatic pilot and putting up with increasing pain.

When you are a frog in hot water, you are seeing the world through a lens created by early traumas.

When you are a frog in hot water, stuck suffering over a prolonged period in a romantic or other kind of relationship or situation (or a series of them, such as a string of jobs), there is always a common denominator: You are seeing the world through a lens or filter that was created by early traumas that restrict your adult perception of the situation.

The reason you're a frog in hot water in that relationship or situation is that, so far, you haven't been able to see beyond the limitations of that lens. Seeing the world through this lens reinforces dysfunctional patterns and keeps you repeating the loop of dysfunctional behaviors that are making you a frog in hot water, suffering with the same unsatisfying results that the dysfunctional behaviors continue producing.

I find it helpful to make an analogy between the lens through which you see the world when you're on automatic pilot and a prison cell with only a tiny window. If you look out through this tiny window, you see very little of the outside world with its possibilities for contentment. If you've never been out of the prison cell, you think that the little bit you see is all that exists, and even if, through the tiny window, you glimpse possibilities for contentment in the outside world, you're still in the prison cell, so your perception is that those possibilities might exist for people "out there," but they are not available to you.

When you're a frog in hot water, you're in the prison cell of your own default programming, and therefore you don't see possibility, you don't create possibilities. But that doesn't mean it's impossible for you to do so!

The reason we stay in an unsatisfying relationship is that our machinery can't choose any of the three doors. When our machinery is running us, we cling to familiar pain at all costs and continue suffering because our perception is that we *need* the relationship and the only way to have it is to pay for it through suffering.

This isn't just true for frog-in-hot-water romantic relationships. It's the same with a frog-in-hot-water situation or series of situations that involve other types of relationships. A friend of mine had the experience of having three promising jobs in a row, all of which soon degenerated into disappointment and frustration. He felt each of his bosses was authoritarian and overly critical.

For eight years, my friend felt like a victim of bad bosses. Then, after quitting his third job, he started to reflect mindfully on his work experiences and to connect them to his childhood with his critical, controlling father. He recognized that, without realizing it, he'd been seeing his bosses through the limiting lens of the anger he felt toward his father, resenting any input his bosses had given him because he'd heard it not as input but as criticism and an unfair need to control him.

My friend had what Jung would call a *father complex,* which made him feel suspicious of and antagonistic toward older men in authority. His way of avoiding being a victim was to fight back with anger, even when fighting back was inappropriate.

After my friend had this insight, he was able to act mindfully and relate positively toward his future employers, in effect, changing his life. He also grew to understand the traumas in his father's childhood that had programmed his father to be so critical and controlling, and he forgave him. His father became supportive and respectful of him, and they started to share good feelings for the first time.

Another way of looking at my friend's experience with his bosses is that it's an example of *transference,* a phenomenon I learned about in therapy. Transference is "the unconscious tendency to assign to others in one's present environment feelings and attitudes associated with significance in one's early life."[1] When we transfer our emotions unconsciously in this way, we're relating to the person in our current life as if he or she were someone from our childhood, and this becomes the lens through which we are experiencing the other person. Years ago, the marriage counselor we went to pointed out to my wife and me that each of us had lost the ability to truly see the other accurately and that, when activated, we each saw the other as our respective mothers instead of seeing and relating to each other as the actual individuals we are.

For me, the biggest problem with transference is its stealth quality. I've found that it's almost impossible in the moment to know that I am truly not talking to the other person but instead seeing the person as my mother and reliving past-based experiences that don't apply in the moment.

Many of us have issues that trigger feelings and interpretations shaped by our early experiences of one or both of our parents and distort our perceptions of current relationships or situations, make us feel like victims or potential victims, and prompt us toward dysfunctional behavior. If you keep having the same unsatisfying experiences and believe there's nothing you can do about it, it's a sign that you're a frog in hot water and that you're seeing the world and yourself through the limited lens of past trauma, whether or not that past trauma involves a complex about your mother, your father, or both of your parents.

The first step toward seeing the bigger picture is recognizing that what you're seeing now is *not* all there is, that the options you believe are your only options are actually only those embedded in your programming. The second step is to recognize that you can develop your ability to dissolve the prison walls and see beyond this limited view to a world of possibility, where you have healthier choices about how you can act and how your actions can lead you to a more satisfying experience of life.

Every time you feel you're in a bind, ask yourself to review the situation as if you're standing outside of it. In reflecting on a situation that upsets me and that I feel trapped in, often I will say to myself "the human that is Steven saw and felt . . ." Then I'll describe what the human that is Steven saw and felt and reflect mindfully on just the facts of what happened instead of on my interpretations of what happened. This allows me to see it without the limiting lens that my programming creates.

Start becoming mindful about your particular limiting lens. Look inside and ask yourself, What is limiting my view of the world when I'm on automatic pilot? Here are some questions to reflect on that will help you answer this question:

- What are my beliefs? My fears? My identity? How do they influence the way I see the world when I allow my machinery to run me?
- How is the limiting lens shaped by a complex or by transference?
- How are all these factors contributing to my feeling in a bind?
- Why am I giving them such power over me? Why do I make them so significant?

Remind yourself to take back your power and to see beyond this limited lens to the world of mindful choices.

You can't solve internal problems by external means.

This means that when it comes to a relationship, you can't expect the other person in the relationship to give you what you're not providing for yourself, and if you do, you're going to be a frog in hot water.

If you don't feel good about yourself and if, instead of parenting yourself, you're looking to the other person to solve the problem, then you're giving away all your power. As a result, how you feel about yourself will be completely dependent on the person's acknowledgment (or lack of acknowledgment) of you. If he or she is acknowledging and loving, you'll feel great; if he or she is disapproving and withholding, you'll feel awful.

I know this experience firsthand. I've only recently come to understand my unrelenting, silent longing for an intimate, romantic relationship and how this longing has driven me to seek in others what I was lacking in myself. Previously I'd felt that if I found the right romantic partner, I'd be complete. I now understand that the hole or void is inside of me and that even the most loving person could not fill that void; I'm the only one that can.

The longing for intimacy in life and relationships is part of being human. It's the way we are wired for connection. But if you enter a relationship with the pattern of wanting the other person to give you what's missing in yourself, the relationship will be a frog-in-hot-water relationship—until you choose Door 1, 2, or 3.

It's helpful to look at the experience of being a frog in hot water as sharing aspects of the five stages of grief.

I've noticed that the experience of being a frog in hot water shares aspects of the five stages of grief that Dr. Elisabeth Kübler-Ross and David Kessler identified as what people experience when faced with imminent death, a theory later adopted to apply to what survivors experience after the loss of a loved one. These stages are denial, anger, bargaining, depression, and acceptance.[2] What follows is a description of what I mean about the relevance of these stages to frog-in-hot-water experiences.

1. **Denial:** I've described how my machinery used to block my experience of pain, which held me captive as a frog in hot water. I believe that all people in frog-in-hot-water situations experience denial about aspects of their situation.

2. **Anger:** The disappointments that arise in relationships can always be traced back to unfulfilled expectations, thwarted intentions, and incomplete communication (things that you didn't express or things that you expressed and the other person hasn't really heard). All of these trigger our upsets and generate anger in relationships. Some people hide this anger from themselves and are unconscious of it; others are consciously angry.

   You cannot be a frog in hot water without having anger either at the other party or yourself and/or the situation itself. As I look back on my life, I see that I shoved that anger into my shadow side, which had the net effect of keeping me in hot water a lot longer, until even my shadow side couldn't hold it, creating a breakdown big enough to have a breakthrough. But even venting the anger doesn't solve the problem. You can be angry for years and still remain a frog in hot water. Simply expressing anger will do nothing; you have to choose Door 1, 2, or 3. But acknowledging and expressing your anger is a stage that can lead to that choice.

3. **Bargaining:** I see bargaining as a handmaiden to denial because it is a strong desire to alter the painful situation by negotiating with an "If I do this, then that . . ." strategy. You are hoping, praying, that things in your relationship will magically change for the better if you approach the problems "this way" instead of "that way."

The clue to why this doesn't work is in the words *magically change*. Bargaining is an activity of your machinery bargaining with itself; while you're negotiating, hoping, and praying for a change, you're remaining on automatic pilot and letting your default programming run you so that you're not making mindful choices about your behavior. I did this a lot, and each time I did, I would tell myself everything would be okay!

It's another prime example of doing the same thing over and over and expecting a different result. I always thought that simply tweaking my actions a bit would do the trick. Again, these little tweaks and an "If I do this, then that . . ." bargaining strategy are very different from making a commitment to acting mindfully to transform the situation by choosing Door 1, 2, or 3.

4. **Depression:** It's par for the course to be depressed about it when you're a frog in hot water.

5. **Acceptance:** What does acceptance mean in this context? Kübler-Ross and Kessler define this last stage in the context of grieving a loved one as accepting the fact that someone you love is no longer physically present and this is how things will be from now on. Thus, in the grieving process, acceptance

is the stage when you accept the new reality and start to go on with your life fully acknowledging and coping with the absence of a loved one.

In terms of frog-in-hot-water situations, acceptance is the last stage as well: It is the stage when you stop denying (or at least stop believing your denials); stop merely being angry about it; stop bargaining (because you finally recognize that mindless bargaining won't work); and stop just being depressed. You accept that you are a frog in hot water.

Of course, in this stage, at times you may still find yourself in denial, you may still be angry, you may still bargain, you may still be depressed, but when you are in the stage of acceptance, you fully acknowledge that you are a frog in hot water.

But whereas grieving cannot bring back a lost loved one, you do have the ability to stop being a frog in hot water. You can choose Door 1—accept the situation fully, warts and all; Door 2—change the situation; or Door 3—remove yourself from the situation.

The stage of accepting the *fact* that you're a frog in hot water doesn't constitute resigning yourself to the situation; it means that you have accepted that being a frog in hot water is your current reality. Only when you reach the point of accepting it as your current reality are you capable of choosing Door 1, 2, or 3.

When I felt the pain in a relationship in the marrow of my bones, that was when I was able to accept that I was a frog in hot water and to use mindfulness to see that I had the right to live life without that pain.

Thus, for frogs in the water as well as for people grieving whose experience Kübler-Ross describes, acceptance is the final stage before going on with the rest of your life. What you do with the rest of your life depends on how you respond after you accept the fact that your current state is as a frog in hot water.

Remember, mindful behavior creates new neural pathways.

Mindful behavior creates new neural pathways, and if you're in a frog-in-hot-water relationship or situation, you can start being mindful right now.

In regard to making mindful choices, it's important to recognize that just exiting through Door 3 and leaving a situation doesn't guarantee that in similar future situations you won't behave in the same ways that you have in the one you just left. If your machinery on automatic pilot triggered you to leave the situation because it could no longer tolerate the situation as it was, then it's more than likely that, even after leaving it, you will still be governed by the same default programming that got you into hot water in the first place. You may breathe a sigh of relief and congratulate yourself on having left the painful situation, but remember this: The only way to avoid a repetition of that situation is by making mindful choices and making them consistently enough to create new neural pathways for healthier behavior.

The crucial point is to know that, even if your machinery has brought you to where you are today rather than your having mindfully brought yourself there, you can start being mindful right now. Furthermore, being mindful means not holding on to judgments.

You are where you are right now; the truth is just the truth. By starting to be mindful now, at this moment, you are creating a better present for yourself and opening yourself up to the world of possibility.

You get the relationship you're ready for.

You get the relationship you're ready for and any relationship built on integrity has the potential to be fulfilling to both people if both people are mindful.

The type of romantic relationship you are drawn to at any given time in your life is determined by the signals that your individual neural circuitry—your Wi-Fi system—sends to and receives from others. If you had a less-than-secure early attachment and your neural circuitry is still the one that was created by your old default programming, you'll be drawn to a relationship that may very well become a frog-in-hot-water relationship.

A terminal relationship is characterized by these three qualities:

1. Both parties are not having their needs met.

2. Both parties are in pain.

3. Both parties have no way of resolving conflicts between them.

A fulfilling relationship is characterized by these three opposite qualities:

1. Both parties are having their needs met.

2. Both parties enjoy the relationship.

3. Both parties can resolve their conflicts.

The goal of having a fulfilling marriage relationship—or friendship, business relationship, or another type of relationship—is achievable as long as both people are willing to be fully self-expressed in the relationship and to use mindfulness to disengage from and dissolve their old programming when it arises.

In achieving the goal of creating a fulfilling relationship, it's important to recognize that if a problem exists, often the true problem is not with the other person but with transference (ghosts of the past that we project onto the current situation and place on the other person).

Another key component to achieving the goal of creating a fulfilling long-term relationship, whether it is a marriage or another kind of long-term relationship, is forgiveness. For a relationship that has had difficult problems in the past to change from unfulfilling to fulfilling, both people have to forgive each other for past actions.

You can't change your behavior overnight.

You can start making mindful choices and acting on them, but the process of becoming more and more mindful happens incrementally, over time. That's why I keep emphasizing both mindfulness and resolve.

Acting mindfully begins with the understanding that the voice in your head isn't you, the logical consequence of which is the decision to be mindful. Being mindful is a never-ending process of disengaging from your machinery. Even after you've made the decision to be mindful, you may be mindful for moments and then go back on automatic pilot. You will remain in that state until you recognize that your programming is running you and you need to stop, interrupt your machinery, focus your mind with intent on being in the present, and start being mindful again. I think of each new time you start being mindful again as a stepping-stone to acting mindfully more often than you act on automatic pilot.

It's helpful to remember the concept of stepping-stones. It's natural, at times, to react to an issue that presses our buttons in a top-down way in which our old neural circuitry is doing the reacting, and the data that's coming in from the present is being held prisoner by the past.[3] But when this happens, it's vital to remember that we can take a Time Out and start to become more mindful. This gives us the ability to dissolve what the top-down voice in our head is telling us and to experience the present without old judgments and interpretations.

The more often we take a Time Out to reflect on our behavior and to start acting mindfully, the less control our old neural circuitry will have in triggering our default behavior, and the more we will develop new neural circuitry that will create healthier behavior.

We need to recognize that maintaining the resolve to accomplish this is a process and that inevitably we will sometimes go back to our old ways and feel our old feelings or variations of them. It's unrealistic to demand or expect that because you begin to see your situation mindfully you will instantly change.

Daniel Siegel, M.D., says that the "natural" state of the "unawakened mind" is to be mindless.[4] Given that we're habituated to mindlessness, it makes perfect sense that we have to train our minds to be mindful and that it takes practice and time to remodel our brains and create new templates.

A metaphor for the process of developing new neural circuitry is the Old Testament story of Moses and his people, after leaving the bondage of slavery in Egypt, wandering through the desert for forty years before they got to the Promised Land. Geographically, it's a relatively short distance to the Promised Land from Egypt, where Moses and the people he led started their journey. Some modern scholars believe that the reason it took forty years was because Moses and his people had a mindset—what I would call a set of Organizing Principles—that came from their slave mentality. Slaves could not develop a new mindset immediately, as shown by the story of creating a golden calf when the people Moses was leading lost faith, fearing that Moses would not come down from Mt. Sinai and believing that their only option was to create a golden idol to pray to in order to save themselves.

This is really the story of the process that would allow the Jews leaving Egypt to run their lives freely in the world of free men. They wandered for four decades—two generations—until the slave mentality died out. It's a story about remodeling the brain at the level of group culture over time, and, on an individual level, a story we can apply to understand dealing with a frog-in-hot-water situation in which, as you've seen, people become enslaved by their default programming.

The story of Moses reminds me to be patient with the process, to maintain my resolve to continue being as mindful as I can, and to recognize that it takes everyone, not just me, time to remodel the brain. This helps me remember to be patient and kind by being a good parent to myself, to not beat myself up, to not shame or blame myself for being human, and to treat others the same way.

By being mindful, I focus my mind on the present and continue to engage in the process of being mindful along my personal journey toward the Promised Land of engagement with the present, emotional balance, and attunement with myself and others. In other words, the sense of well-being that comes with healthier behavior.

You must act on what you've learned and start using mindfulness to change your behavior.

Learning to be aware of the specific content of your default programming and understanding how your past experiences caused it has no value unless you act on what you've learned and start using mindfulness to change your behavior.

You can use your intellect to search for all the causes of your unhappiness and still not do anything about mindfully changing your behavior and remodeling your brain. *Only you can change you.* Don't let the search to understand yourself become a distraction from recognizing that ultimately why you are the way you are is less important than the productiveness of using mindful awareness to create the change that will, in turn, create a happier life for yourself.

Every moment in your life can be a wonderful teacher—but only if you focus your mind with intent on the present and choose to act mindfully. Don't waste a moment on regret. Regret is just another aspect of shame and blame, and it comes from your default programming. Regret focuses on the past, which is history. Right now, you are exactly where you are supposed to be. Right now, this moment, there is only the present and the future, and if you decide to be mindful, it is filled with possibility!

···················· PAUSE YOUR MACHINERY ····················

- Review the list of seven lessons and mindfully reflect on them one at a time to help you see where you are regarding the relationship or situation you've identified as being, or potentially becoming, a frog-in-hot-water experience. For example, what lens are you seeing the relationship or situation through that is keeping you in it and triggering you to act the way you are acting?

  - Are you experiencing transference, as we've defined the term in this chapter?

  - Are you looking for someone else to solve what is really your problem and upset with that person because he or she is not solving it for you?

  - Are you in denial about your pain or other aspects of the relationship or situation? Are you bargaining? Are you angry? Are you depressed? Have you accepted that it is a frog-in-hot-water relationship or situation?

- If you're in a frog-in-hot-water relationship, does it have the three qualities of a terminal relationship (both parties are not having their needs met; both are in pain; and both have no way of resolving conflicts between them)? If so, have you and the other party recognized the possibility to change it to being a fulfilling relationship (both parties are having their needs met; both enjoy the relationship; both can resolve their conflicts)?

- Write a description of where you are on the journey from intellectually being aware of how your programming is putting you in a frog-in-hot-water or potentially frog-in-hot-water relationship or situation to behaving in a new, mindful way that will create the possibility of fulfillment instead of pain.

- If you haven't started acting mindfully to change your behavior, describe in your notebook or computer file what is preventing you from doing so. Now describe what you need to do in order to make mindful choices about it.

In the next two chapters, I'll share with you practices that develop mindfulness, gratitude, and loving-kindness and that increase my ability to stay mindful even in situations that get me activated. I'll also share with you insights I've found particularly inspiring, to motivate you in the process of using your mind to transform your brain and change your life.

Part IV

TOOLS AND TECHNIQUES

FOR A HAPPIER,

HEALTHIER LIFE

CHAPTER EIGHTEEN

DECREASING ANXIETY, INCREASING GRATITUDE, MINDFULNESS, LOVING-KINDNESS, AND WELL-BEING

····· 🧠 ·····

Here are practices and exercises I use to support me in being mindful and inventing myself anew by remodeling my brain so that I'll stop acting in dysfunctional ways and instead act in ways that make me happier. I hope they will be as helpful to you as they are to me.

Practicing Breathing to Alleviate Anxiety

I tend to be oblivious of my true feelings when I'm activated, and I create anxiety to cover those feelings. I've found that an antidote for this anxiety and a way to get in touch with my underlying real feelings is to do a breathing exercise instead of going into a dead zone and being taken over by the anxiety.

The breathing exercise I'm about to share with you will help you alleviate your anxiety.

Let me introduce it by saying I've learned that part of inventing myself anew is learning to love myself, and this means learning to direct my natural soothing resources (we all have these resources inside of us) toward myself, both the little child in me, with all the fears from my childhood, and the adult who is embracing the power I have to change. In reinventing myself, I'm learning that it's all right to give myself love, compassion, tenderness, and care, all of which my self-critic makes it challenging for me to do. I'm also learning to stay connected to the fulfillment I feel in moving forward with my life and allowing myself peace.

All of this comes back to learning to honor my feelings. It's impossible to be at peace within ourselves or with others if we don't honor our feelings!

Now, to the exercise.

BREATHING EXERCISE ·······································

1. First, pay attention to your anxiety by noticing your breathing and scan your body for any signs that tell you that you are anxious. Ask yourself: Where am I tense? Is my breathing labored? Am I holding my breath?

2. Second, look within to find which emotion or emotions are linked to or are being covered by the anxiety: Is it love, anger, guilt, or grief? Is it the subset of pain and longing?

3. Third, sit straight in a chair or lie down and breathe in through your mouth for two counts, hold your breath for two counts, and then exhale for four counts. Repeat the exercise three or

four times, filling your belly on the inhale and releasing all the air on the exhale.

When you're anxious, I suggest you take a few moments to follow these steps, remembering to repeat the exercise three or four times, as I do. Mindfully fill your belly as you inhale and release all the air as you exhale.

After you're comfortable doing this for a count of two, you may want to move up to inhaling for three counts, holding for three, then exhaling for six counts. You may eventually move up to inhaling for a longer time if that feels good to you, and always remember to follow it with a double count on exhaling. Choose the count that works best for you.

If you practice this exercise it will soon become natural, and it will keep you relaxed and able to reduce anxiety when it bubbles up.

You may find yourself resisting the idea of doing the breathing exercise, but remember, it's all part of learning to love yourself! Why would you want to be anxious if there's a way to reduce your anxiety? Your being doesn't want to be anxious; your anxiety, when in the case of an actual threat being absent, is all part of the fight or flight system that your machinery and your default programming needlessly call into action at the expense of your peace of mind and health.

Practicing Gratitude

Gratitude, opening your heart in appreciation, is a wonderful feeling: It feels good physically, and it feels good mentally and emotionally. With its constant search for problems that may not even exist, my default programming is fabulous at making me worry rather than focusing on all the good things to be grateful about. Practicing feeling gratitude is part of learning to be mindful and to feel good about myself and the world, to be in the present instead of remaining in my fear-dominated past.

Here's the gratitude exercise my therapist Robin L. Kay, Ph.D., gave me to help me create a new template for gratitude. Practicing this is an effective way of reprogramming yourself to create new neural pathways for positive feelings and behavior.

GRATITUDE EXERCISE

1. Name ten things in your life you feel grateful for.
2. Now, one at a time, say to yourself silently each of the things you are grateful for (notice the physical sensations you experience as you feel grateful for it). For example, you might silently say to yourself, "I'm grateful for my health, I'm grateful I have a house to live in, I'm grateful I am not in a war-torn country, I'm grateful I am not impoverished."
3. Think mindfully and really feel the gratefulness for each item.
4. Do this every day and keep searching for additional items each time to expand yourself, your positive feelings, and your creativity.

Practicing Mindful Meditation

Many years ago I was doing a research project on success in various fields, and I was fortunate to interview Ram Dass, the spiritual teacher who wrote, among other books, *Be Here Now*, a classic book for Western readers on spirituality, meditation, and yoga. As part of the book, Ram Dass wrote about his transformation from Richard Alpert, who had gotten a Ph.D. in psychology from Stanford, then taught at Harvard, to Baba Ram Dass, the name he took while studying in India with his Hindu guru, Neem Karoli Baba, who taught him meditation. During our interview, I asked Ram Dass what his experience of meditation was like. He described his meditation practice, which was sometimes hours long, as "a concentration exercise where you develop very powerful concentration, like a laser beam."[1]

Although the meditation practice I'm recommending is for 5 or 10 minutes to half an hour, the practice is still the same as the one Ram Dass described to me. He talked about sitting with your eyes closed and "focusing on the muscle in your abdomen rising and falling with each breath. All you do is watch it rise and fall, and you notice the quality of its rising and the quality of its falling . . ."[2]

I mentioned earlier (in Chapter 10, when I introduced the concept of mindfulness meditation) that when you close your eyes and start observing your breath, thoughts are going to come into your head; that's normal. You just let them go and return your focus to your breath. Ram Dass described it this way:

Every time a thought comes, you notice what the thought was. Instead of following the thought, you come right back to your breath until your mind gives up and it just stays on the breath. It doesn't go anywhere. Up until then, you sit down, you start to follow your breath, and your mind is thinking, "For this I got a Ph.D.?" or "My knee hurts," or

"When is lunch?" or "What kind of Mickey Mouse thing is this?" These are all thoughts. The teachers . . . always say, "Whatever arises, notice it, then return your awareness to your breath." . . . After a while, what happens is you cultivate a part of your brain, or a part of your awareness, that just is. It's just sitting, watching it all come and go.[3]

Talking about the rewards of meditation practice, Ram Dass shared the following observation, which coincides with what I've shared with you about being mindful and dis-identifying with your past-based programming and becoming truly present: "When you realize the way in which your mind is creating your universe, the way in which your childhood and my childhood have all led us to be having a different experience at this moment, and then you start to learn how to go inside in your mind and get behind your own thought forms and break the identification, it gets so exciting and so breathtaking. The meditative practices changed my life."[4]

I think the most challenging part of meditation is making it a priority. Our lives are so full of things we feel we have to do it's difficult to commit to setting aside time to meditate. If you've never meditated before, you may also experience a resistance to doing something new, akin to fear of the unknown. You may be intimidated, and think, "Well, maybe other people can do this, but I don't know if I can." This is why I found Ram Dass's comments on his meditation practice—especially the kinds of thoughts that passed through his head—so helpful. They let you know that it really is normal for thoughts to come into your head as you attempt to quiet your mind and concentrate on your breathing. They remind you that part of being mindful is not judging yourself for your thoughts, in fact, not judging your meditation.

Meditating is a process; it's not a contest, and it's impossible to do it wrong! Just experience it; don't judge yourself as doing it "well" or "badly." It's all part of the process of learning to keep dissolving the thoughts that enter your mind as you keep focusing on the present, which, in the case of meditating, is focusing on your breath.

A friend once told me, "I don't really like meditation, but I guess it's better than sitting around doing nothing." Given that research shows that doing mindfulness meditation increases your ability to be mindful in other situations in your life, it's a *lot* better to practice mindfulness meditation than to sit around doing nothing!

MINDFUL MEDITATION EXERCISE

1. Sit straight on a chair in a darkened room. Close your eyes, breathe naturally, and relax your entire body, letting go of all tension in your face, neck, legs, arms, and feet.

2. When you feel your body is relaxed, start to focus on your breath. I do this by focusing my attention on my abdomen rising and falling. Focus on breathing in and breathing out. Notice the thoughts that come into your head, and instead of holding on to them or judging yourself for having them, keep returning your focus to your breath. Experience this for the time that you've allotted for it.

I recommend starting your meditation practice by doing a mindfulness meditation for 5 or 10 minutes, or, if you want to, up to half an hour. My experience with meditation is that the more I've meditated, the more I want to meditate. It relaxes me as well as helps me to be mindful and more present in my daily life.

I've mentioned that I took a course in mindfulness meditation at UCLA. If you'd like to do a guided meditation in which someone leads you through a meditation, the UCLA Mindful Awareness Research Center has made several user-friendly meditations available online. Go to http://marc.ucla.edu/body.cfm?id=29 and click the "Guided Meditations" tab.

I generally do my meditation when my day is done, when I'm ready for bed. Prior to creating this practice, I would fall asleep watching television. Now I find that I get so much benefit from the peace that comes with meditating that it feels almost barbaric to spoil the tranquility with mindless television afterwards. Meditating adds a very restful quality to my life as I come to the close of each day.

Practicing Loving-Kindness

I've found this meditation practice from the UCLA Mindful Awareness Research Center to be extremely beneficial for my outlook and emotional state. As the designers of the exercise explain: "Science has shown the importance of cultivating positive emotions for our general sense of well-being. Loving-kindness is an excellent complement of the mindfulness practice. Loving-kindness is a natural quality of our heart and mind that can be accessible at any moment. It is not syrupy sweet, nor inauthentic; it is more an unconditional wish that you or another could be happy. You can generate this quality by bringing to mind someone you love and feeling in your body what that sensation is like. You can then increase [it] and [let it] pervade [your being] by wishing someone well."[5]

The exercise is very simple. Just follow these instructions.

LOVING-KINDNESS EXERCISE

1. Sit straight on a chair in a darkened room. Close your eyes, breathe naturally, and relax your entire body, letting go of all the tension in your race, neck, legs, arms, and feet.

2. Focus your mind on someone you love. Picture that person and feel your love for him or her in your body, attuning yourself to what you are really feeling. Don't pretend and don't push your feelings of love; just let them flow.

3. Now wish the person well by sending him or her positive thoughts about specific things you wish for that individual, such as happiness and health. Wish anything positive that comes to mind. If the person is facing specific challenges, send him or her positive thoughts about overcoming those challenges.

4. Now focus on you and send positive wishes to yourself. If you've never done this before, it may be challenging; you might feel self-conscious, and judgments may arise about sending positive wishes to and for yourself. Do your best to be mindful, to let go of whatever judgments come up, and open your heart to you so that you can experience yourself lovingly and feel that it's fine for you to send positive wishes to yourself. I have experienced that I get better with this over time.

5. Now focus on sending positive wishes to people in your life with whom you are having difficulty. When I do this part of the loving-kindness exercise, I picture the person in my mind, do my best to be mindful, let go of my judgments, and see if I can open my heart to that person and experience him or her from the COAL state of curiosity, openness, acceptance, and love. If I feel my heart opening to the person, I send him or her positive wishes. If I don't, I just go as far as I can go authentically and let it go. And then, on another day, I do it again, and I just experience whatever I experience on that day, too. I find that over time I am able to have more love even for the difficult people in my life. This makes it easier for me to interact with them and it increases my own sense of well-being.

The following insights by the UCLA Mindful Awareness Research Center are extremely helpful in doing this loving-kindness practice: "You are encouraged to be creative with this practice and stay connected to your inner experience. If you don't feel it, don't think this is a problem. This practice takes time and can be viewed like planting seeds that will ripen sometime in the future. It is very common for people to easily send loving-kindness to someone they love but have difficulty sending it to themselves or to difficult people in their lives."[6]

Here are some phrases that the designers of the exercise suggest you use in sending positive wishes:

- May you/I be happy and peaceful.
- May you/I be healthy and strong.

- May you/I be safe from all danger.
- May you/I have ease and well-being in your life.[7]

To me, the key points to remember as you do this exercise are these: (1) Only experience whatever it is that you are authentically experiencing; (2) every time you do it, you are "planting seeds"; and (3) it takes time, and if you continue doing the practice, these seeds will blossom into the good feelings that come with loving-kindness. As with all meditative practices, it's important that each time you practice, you let go of all judgments as they come up.

···················· PAUSE YOUR MACHINERY ····················

- Think mindfully about how each of the tools and techniques in this chapter might benefit you. Can you commit to practicing at least one of them? Write down how you see yourself using one or more of them in your daily life. If you decide to commit to meditating and/or doing the loving-kindness exercise now, write down what time of day you will do your practice, and how long you will devote to it.

In the next chapter, I'll present you with a method I've developed that's very effective in helping me interrupt my machinery and start to act mindfully, especially when I'm feeling confused or upset.

CHAPTER NINETEEN

CREATING YOUR WISDOM PAGES

..... 🧠 .....

Each time I've gotten a new understanding that I feel has helped me, I've made note of it in a file I refer to as my "Wisdom Pages." I keep refining the information, and, at times of stress, I go directly to these Wisdom Pages to use as an operating manual, a list of basic life rules and insights into my inner world that support me in owning my programming rather than it owning me. When I feel confused or upset, I read my Wisdom Pages to get perspective and remind myself of what I've learned!

I think of my Wisdom Pages as a type of *exoskeleton.* Ordinarily we think of an exoskeleton as the hard shell of an animal like a crab or a lobster that functions as its external support and protection. But the term is also used to describe external means of support for people with physical disabilities. In this context, an exoskeleton is "a prosthetic device in which support is provided by an outside structure (not an implant), such as an artificial limb."[1] I recommend creating your own Wisdom Pages and using them as an exoskeleton to support you in acting mindfully in your daily life.

The Pause Your Machinery exercises you've done as you read this book provide you with an excellent resource for the information you want to record in your Wisdom Pages. A great place to start compiling life lessons is with the Guiding Principles you created to replace your old, dysfunctional Organizing Principles. (Refresh your memory by reviewing Chapter 11.) Notice, for example, that in my Wisdom Pages I've included my Guiding Principles "Feelings aren't facts" and "You can't argue with another person's perceptions," among others, to remind me to disengage from my Operating Principles and the dysfunctional acts they trigger.

Your descriptions of the core issues, beliefs, and fears embedded in your programming are a rich resource from which to choose the insights about yourself that you want to include in your Wisdom Pages to help you interrupt your machinery and instead make mindful choices.

I suggest that you keep your Wisdom Pages short enough—one to six pages only—so that you can read them easily when you have a few spare minutes or are feeling confused or upset. I also recommend revising your Wisdom Pages as you learn new life lessons or want to focus on different aspects of your behavior you want to change. Perhaps you will want to retain your former Wisdom Pages in an archive to review periodically to help you trace your progress in becoming more and more mindfully aware.

Here are the most recent Wisdom Pages I prepared for myself as an example to help you create your own exoskeleton to support your practice of mindful awareness.

MY WISDOM PAGES

- We are reaction machines. We cannot *not* react; it is how we are designed. The choice we have is how we relate to what is happening, whether we will react on automatic pilot or respond mindfully.
- When you're on automatic pilot, the brain will do what is familiar even when it is useless or destructive.
- The first step toward enlightenment is recognizing that the voice in your head is not you.
- Trauma affects the brain by embedding the belief that there is no world outside its traumatized universe.
- My core issues are abandonment and attachment issues.
- My childhood trauma frightened me into keeping away from my painful feelings.
- When I'm on automatic pilot, my default programming uses thinking to push feelings away and it covers them with anxiety.
- Being anxious or numb is a signal that I'm being run by my default programming. If I feel anxious, I must remind myself to simply breathe.
- Put the past in the past. Create a future to live into or else I will just relive the past!
- Life is filled with possibility.
- The positive future you are living into gives you a positive feeling in the present.
- Conversations about possibility are Kryptonite for the default programming.
- Possibility has no shelf life. Act mindfully to create possibility today!
- Honor myself by being fully self-expressed.

- It's all about *choosing*. Choosing means mindfully figuring out what you want and then choosing it with 100 percent of yourself. When you choose, you live passionately!
- Feelings take priority. Don't use thoughts to push away feelings.
- Defenses serve just one purpose: to block feelings. The defense of denial is my worst enemy. Ruminating on an issue is also a defense; it inhibits growth by keeping you in the loop of your default programming.
- I need to parent myself better. I've been punishing myself with guilt that turns into anxiety and creates isolation for having feelings of rage toward Mom and Dad. Instead, I should see the anxiety for what it is: a product of this guilt. Remember, these murderous feelings are not a crime. They are my legitimate response to how I was treated! And now it is the present, and if I am mindfully aware, I can feel my anger about the past and resolve it and parent myself mindfully in the present.
- Experience joy by allowing yourself to actually *feel* pleasure. Let it fill you up; bring it to every cell of your body.
- Focus on gratitude. Do the gratitude exercise every day.
- Comfort comes from facing feelings directly. Putting intellect ahead of emotional experience prevents calming and soothing yourself. Look within to your deepest and very important feelings.
- Pain and suffering are better than being in a state of anesthetization.
- Embrace my own sadness instead of pushing it away.
- Whenever I'm fearless, I'm at my best, and fearless means that I acknowledge my fears and then act anyway!
- When I'm desperate, I've lost all my power.

- Be like a strong tree in the forest that doesn't need anyone. If you don't *need* people, the people who are in your life are people you *choose* to be there.

- Love is simply acceptance—accepting the way someone is and the way someone is not.

- My mother's eyes toward me as a child were ignoring, neglectful, and dismissive, and I've unconsciously done the same to myself and others. It's essential that I start noticing this unconscious, self-destructive attitude toward myself and other people. Stop simply going through the motions in my important relationships and truly care about myself and others.

- I have difficulty having compassion for others if they are angry with me or want something from me. Practice expanding my capacity for real heartfelt compassion.

- When I'm not mindful, I'm not authentic in my relationships because everything I do is to keep the relationships safe, alive, so as not to have people mad at me. My answer to creating better relationships is to recognize that relationships simply are and that I don't have to suppress my feelings and self-expression for them. Just be and let everyone else be.

- Get clear about what I want; choose, take a stand, commit, and don't sell out to my machinery.

- Give myself permission to feel angry when anger is the appropriate response to how someone is acting toward me.

- My default programming equates disappointing someone with harming them. This is false. If I act on this false belief I'm not honoring myself because I don't feel I have the right to do what I want or to receive what I want.

- You don't need to "deserve" or be "entitled to" to want what you want.
- It's all right to say "no." Three statements will always allow me to mindfully respond to requests I want to say "no" to:
  - I don't want to.
  - I don't feel like it.
  - It's my life.
- You cannot solve internal issues by external means. You can't look to material things or other people to raise your self-esteem.
- I can only change myself. I can't fix or change others. It's not my responsibility or my ability.
- I go back and forth from adult to child. Stop this by being in the moment, with fresh eyes, and no automatics.
- I get caught up in my own stuff when I'm on automatic pilot, which frustrates others who feel I don't care about them and causes them to turn off on me—and I don't have a clue that they have done it or why.
- Don't avoid conflict; that leads to going dead/numb. Relationships thrive because people take risks and face important feelings. Strive for full self-expression as the door to authenticity, integrity, and fulfillment.
- Feelings aren't facts. Listen mindfully, feel your feelings, and speak mindfully, without judgment, without shaming and blaming.
- You can't argue with another person's perceptions.
- You get what you want by enrolling the other person in your point of view by sharing yourself and the possibilities you see in a way that inspires!

- Play everything in life with the love of the game!
- As Eleanor Roosevelt said, "Do one thing every day that scares you." Do random acts of kindness and regular acts of courage.
- All the insights and life lessons in the world have no value unless you act on what you've learned and start using mindfulness to change your behavior.

PAUSE YOUR MACHINERY

- In a new file or notebook, create your first set of Wisdom Pages. Start by writing down some or all of the Guiding Principles you created to support you in acting mindfully instead of being run by your programming. Also include observations about your core issues, what triggers your programming, and how you act in various situations in which you become activated if you're on automatic pilot. Include, too, some of the important insights and information you want to repeat silently or aloud to yourself in these situations.

Remember to make your Wisdom Pages file or notebook six pages or fewer, and summarize each nugget of wisdom about life and about yourself as clearly and briefly as possible.

The act of writing your Wisdom Pages will help you learn the life lessons that you are teaching yourself in your process of self-transformation. And every time you read your Wisdom Pages, you will be encouraging yourself to become more and more mindful.

As we've seen, living mindfully takes continuing effort and, therefore, continuing resolve, but the rewards are tremendous, especially when you consider the alternative of living within the limitations of life on automatic pilot. In the concluding chapter, I want to share with you a few simple ways to think about these basic issues in your daily life and to stay on the path of mindfulness.

CONCLUSION

MY SHORTHAND MESSAGES FOR YOU TO LIVE A LIFE OF AUTHENTICITY AND ALIVENESS

····· 🧠 ·····

We can live our lives mindfully or on automatic pilot. The more we are mindful, the greater our sense of well-being, the more nurturing our relationships will be, the more able we will be to accomplish our goals, and the more joy and fulfillment we will experience.

The more we live mindlessly by repeating our past-based dysfunctional behavior, the more we will be in denial, the more we will rationalize and justify our self-defeating behavior, the more we will create frog-in-hot-water relationships, and the more helpless we will feel to resolve problems.

The choice is simple: Living on automatic pilot puts us in the dead zone, where we may think we're alive, but, because we're not really present—that is, *not* here in the now—we're still trapped in the past, wondering why the stress and frustration and suffering we're experiencing is so much like the stress and frustration and suffering we've experienced before.

When we're functioning mindlessly, without challenging the voice in our head and the feelings that the voice tells us are facts, we can never truly live with power and integrity.

Without mindful awareness, we don't recognize that the reason we keep having the same feelings over and over again is because we're creating them by thinking and acting in the same ways we did in the past. We don't recognize that we're letting our hardwiring run us instead of interrupting our machinery and focusing our mind on the present so that we can make mindful choices that will create new neural pathways for healthier behavior. When we live mindfully, instead of living in the dead zone, we live a life of aliveness and authenticity.

The challenge for us is to overcome the habits of thinking and acting that are embedded in our default programming. Our machinery is territorial and doesn't want to change its programming, so in order to transform ourselves not only do we have to interrupt our machinery and start making mindful choices, we also have to keep doing it again and again until it becomes more and more natural for us to do so. The machinery doesn't want to give up easily; in fact, it doesn't want to give up at all. At some point—perhaps only moments after you've become mindful and interrupted your machinery—it will reengage you in your old programming again. For this reason, you need to be vigilant and to pursue your commitment to interrupting your machinery, focusing on the present, and once again becoming mindful.

Remember my Guiding Principle "Every time something new happens, I go back to my old ways"? It helps me to realize that if old familiar thoughts and feelings come up again—which they will—in whatever new situation I find myself, it's because my machinery is kidnapping me, and that, because it's kidnapping me, I'm starting to act dysfunctionally. It reminds me that in order to live a life of aliveness and joy I need to become mindfully aware and interrupt my machinery instead of allowing it to run me.

A major part of the process of transforming ourselves is to continually dissolve interpretations and judgments and develop empathy for ourselves as well as for others. Often when we're on automatic pilot, instead of having empathy, we judge others for not being the way we think they should be and we judge ourselves for not being the way we think we should be.

A vivid example of how empathy dissolves judgmental thinking about ourselves and others, and how mindfulness helps us develop empathy, is our reaction to a child we're meeting for the first time. If we walk into the home of new friends and find their child is having a tantrum directed at its parents, our automatic reaction may be to become upset and judgmental of both the child and the parents. If the parents tell us the child is autistic, our attitude immediately changes. We become mindful and have compassion and empathy for the child and the parents now that we realize that the child is acting that way because of his or her wiring.

Instead of being judgmental of ourselves, if we look at the dysfunctional ways in which we currently act as the result of our wiring from the past, we will see ourselves with compassion and empathy, and we can resolve to change our behavior to be more constructive.

It's the same with our experience of other people: If we see their dysfunctional behavior as the logical progression of a kind of wiring that's different from ours, we will have compassion and empathy for them. In addition, we will seek to become more attuned to them.

This doesn't prohibit us from expressing how we would like to improve our relationships with others; it just means that we will start the conversation from a state of mindfulness rather than from judgment, shame, and blame, which can end a conversation before it really begins.

As we've discussed, when we're on automatic pilot, we also often judge whatever we're experiencing against our expectation—our picture—of what our experience "should be." When this happens, with our machinery running us, our disappointment cues us to feel bad rather than to look at the situation mindfully and to let go of our interpretations and judgments.

When we're on automatic pilot, we may complain about the experiences that we want and don't currently have instead of mindfully reflecting on the possibility that our disappointment is an outcome of our current wiring. The reality is that our current wiring enables us to do certain things very well and other things not as well, and that our attitude about how we see this results in our experience of the situation. We can choose to see it as "good" or "bad" when, in reality, it isn't good or bad, it's just "what is" at that second. We always have the opportunity to remind ourselves that:

I'm having the experience I'm having right now because I'm on automatic pilot, which is cueing my old programmed behavior.

I will commit to being mindful so that, in this moment, I can change my action to a mindful one. Over time, I will transform my wiring to create better and better experiences for myself, to stop judging myself, and, instead, to lovingly accept myself.

I think of this as analogous to the story of "the ugly duckling" that never felt it belonged until it chanced upon a group of beings that looked just like it did. Then it recognized it wasn't an *ugly* duckling; it was something different—a beautiful swan. In order to develop empathy for ourselves, we have to stop comparing ourselves to our picture of how we "should be" and instead cherish our uniqueness. To develop empathy for others, we have to stop comparing them to our picture of how they "should be," and we will then start to cherish their uniqueness. We are all as we should be at this very moment, and at this very moment, we all have the potential to continue growing.

Whenever people ask me the generic question "How are you?" I always mention that I'm the perfect example of me, and sometimes I follow up with, "And can you believe that both my dogs have coats with a perfect fit as well?"

I mentioned earlier that I had the privilege of interviewing the spiritual teacher Ram Dass. At one point in our interview, he talked about his experience of how, through the mindfulness that he was developing through meditation, he was gaining a different perspective on his identity and all the other aspects of his programming that earlier in his life he thought of as all of who he was. He told me, "There's another part of me that has nothing to do with that."[1]

When I asked him about his personal definition of success, he said: "I'd say it's awakening to your full potential as a human being, realizing that I am what I can be, not by criteria of money, power, fame—that all comes and goes—but just in the sense that I can feel the depths of my compassion now. I can feel the depths of the emptiness in my being. I can feel the depth of the joy and fun and play. I can feel my fears and desires . . . It's as if I'm awakening just as fast as I can. It's just going on."[2]

I believe this is the definition of success for all of us: awakening to our full potential as human beings. Wherever you are on the journey, you are the perfect you at this moment, awakening to your full potential as a human being.

The way I think of this for myself is that the human that I am at this moment has no alternative to the process of "bumping into walls." The human being that I am also has no alternative but to continue awakening.

My five shorthand messages for you as you embark on this journey are these:

1. Be mindful.
2. Remember that the voice in your head isn't you.
3. Remember that feelings aren't facts.
4. Quiet the voice in your head.
5. Remember that the process of self-transformation is "gain it, lose it, gain it again!" Remember that all of the insight, all of the "aha"s, come to us when we are mindfully aware. The key to awakening is remembering that sometimes we will be mindful and sometimes we will go back on automatic pilot

again, and there's no way to prevent an overload of the system that temporarily sends us back to our default position. This is the state of being human!

The goal is to spend more and more time being mindful and less and less time being run by your machinery. Now it's up to you!

·········· PAUSE YOUR MACHINERY ··········

- Write a description of your personal and professional goals.
- Keeping in mind the information you've learned about your programming and about changing your brain to change your life, describe in writing the specific areas in which being mindful is particularly challenging for you and the steps you're going to take (or are already taking) in order to be mindful and to accomplish your goals.
- Write down the mindful step you're going to take right now to support you in accomplishing one or more of your goals.

I wish you great success, happiness, and above all, freedom.

NOTES

Introduction

1. *60 Minutes,* untitled episode (February 10, 2013).

Chapter One

1. Sam Wang, *The Neuroscience of Everyday Life (The Great Courses)* DVD-ROM Course Guidebook (Princeton: Princeton University, 2010): 1.

2. National Center for Biotechnology Information, "Decade of the Brain: An Agenda for the Nineties," *Western Journal of Medicine* 161(3), September 1994, http://www.ncbi.nlm.nih.gov/pubmed/7975560.

3. Christi Parsons, "Obama Calls for Funding for Brain Science Initiative," *Los Angeles Times,* April 2, 2013, http://www.latimes.com/news/politics/la-pn -obama-funding-brain-mapping-20130402,0,7490745.story.

4. Christopher Chabris and Daniel Simons, "Using Just 10% of Your Brain? Think Again," *The Wall Street Journal,* November 16, 2012, http://online .wsj.com/article/SB10001424127887324556304578119351875421218 .html?ll_leid=207&refer=4002.

5. Abigail Tucker, "Born to Be Mild," *The Smithsonian,* January 2013, http://www .smithsonianmag.com/science-nature/Are-Babies-Born-Good-183837741.html.

6. U.S. Department of Health and Human Services, Office of Population Affairs, Adolescent Family Life Self-Directed Module, "Maturation of Pre-frontal Cortex," http://www.hhs.gov/opa/familylife/tech_assistance/etraining /adolescent_brain/Development/prefrontal_cortex/.

7. Charles Duhigg, *The Power of Habit* (New York: Random House, 2012).

8. Definition from MedicineNet.com.

Chapter Two

1. "Harry F. Harlow," Muskingum University, Department of Psychology, muskingum.edu/~psych/psycweb/history/harlow.htm.

Chapter Five

1. This theory is the "triune brain theory" (*triune* meaning three parts), developed by Paul MacLean, former director of the Laboratory of the Brain and Behavior at the United States National Institute of Mental Health. Renate N. Caine and Geoffrey Caine, *Making Connections: Teaching and the Human Brain* (Nashville, TN: Incentive Publications, 1990). Accessed online at http://www.buffalostate .edu/orgs/bcp/brainbasics/triune.html.

2. Ibid.

3. Ibid.

4. Ibid.

5. Ibid.

6. Daniel J. Siegel, M.D., *The Mindful Brain: The Neurobiology of Well-Being*, CD-ROM (Louisville, CO: Sounds True, Inc.): Disc 1.

7. Andrew Curran, *The Little Book of Big Stuff About the Brain: The True Story of Your Amazing Brain* (Bethel, CT: Crown House, 2008): 135.

8. Ibid.

9. Ibid., 137.

10. Ibid., 139.

11. Ibid., 141.

12. Ibid.

13. Ibid., 139.

14. Ibid., 143.

15. Ibid.

16. Ibid.

17. Ibid., 146.

18. Ibid., 148–49.

19. Ibid., 148–51.

20. Ibid., 151.

21. Definitions from MedicineNet.com.

22. Curran, *About the Brain,* 151–55.

23. James L. Fosshage, "Fundamental Pathways to Change: Illuminating Old and Creating New Relationship Experience." Paper presented at the XII International Forum of IFPS, May 22-23, 2002, Oslo, Norway; c 2003 Taylor & Francis. Accessed at http://jamesfosshage.com/articles/Fosshage -Fundamental_Pathways-2003.pdf.

24. Curran, *About the Brain,* 155.

25. Quote was included in a book review by Laura Landro of *The Emotional Life of Your Brain* by Richard J. Davidson and Sharon Begley, *The Wall Street Journal,* March 5, 2012, http://online.wsj.com/article/SB1000142405297020457140457 7257713834265838.html.

26. Stephanie M. Lee, "Berkeley Center Awards Grants to Study Gratitude," *San Francisco Chronicle* (December 5, 2012): Section D, 1,3.

27. Steven J. Fogel with Mark Bruce Rosin, *My Mind Is Not Always My Friend* (Los Angeles: Fresh River Press, 2010).

28. Ibid.

Chapter Six

1. Daniel J. Siegel, *The Developing Mind: How Relationships and the Brain Interact to Shape Who We Are* (New York: Guilford Press, 2001), 221.

2. Siegel, *Mindful Brain,* CD-ROM, Disc 1.

3. Ibid.

4. Ibid., Discs 1–4.

5. Siegel, *Developing Mind.* Quote found online at Goodreads, http://www .goodreads.com/work/quotes/392414-the-developing-mind-toward-a -neurobiology-of-interpersonal-experience.

6. Siegel, *Mindful Brain,* CD-ROM, Disc 1.

7. Daniel J. Siegel, M.D., "Reflections on the Mindful Brain: A Brief Overview Adapted from *The Mindful Brain: Reflection and Attunement in the Cultivation of Well-Being* (New York: W.W. Norton, 2007)," http://www.lifespanlearn.org /documents/Siegel-article.pdf, 14.

8. Siegel, *Mindful Brain*, CD-ROM, Disc 1.

9. Ibid.

10. Ibid.

11. Ibid.

12. Ibid., Discs 1, 4.

13. Siegel, *Reflections*, 5.

14. Siegel, *Mindful Brain*, CD-ROM, Disc 1.

15. Siegel, *Reflections*, 13.

Chapter Seven

1. Siegel, *Reflections*, 10–11.

2. Ibid.

3. Siegel, *Developing Mind*. Quote found online at Goodreads, http://www .goodreads.com/work/quotes/392414-the-developing-mind-toward-a -neurobiology-of-interpersonal-experience.

4. Siegel, *Mindful Brain*, CD-ROM, Disc 1.

5. Ibid.

6. Ibid., Disc 3.

7. Ibid., Discs 1, 3.

Chapter Eight

1. Siegel, *Mindful Brain*, CD-ROM, Disc 3.

2. Ibid.

3. Ibid.

4. Ibid.

5. Jeff Hawkins and Sandra Blakeslee, *On Intelligence* (New York: Henry Holt, 2004), 42.

6. Siegel, *Mindful Brain*, CD-ROM, Disc 3.

7. Ibid.

8. Ibid.

Chapter Nine

1. Siegel, *Reflections*, 12.

2. Ibid.

3. Siegel, *Mindful Brain*, CD-ROM, Disc 1.

4. Ibid.

5. Ibid.

6. Siegel, *Reflections*, 12.

7. Siegel, *Mindful Brain*, CD-ROM, Disc 1.

8. Ibid.

9. Siegel, *Reflections*, 12.

10. Siegel, *Mindful Brain*, CD-ROM, Discs 1, 3.

11. Siegel, *Developing Mind*. Quote found online at Goodreads, http://www
.goodreads.com/work/quotes/392414-the-developing-mind-toward-a
-neurobiology-of-interpersonal-experience.

12. Siegel, *Reflections*, 12.

13. Ibid.

14. Diane Ackerman, "The Brain on Love," *The New York Times,* Opinionator,
March 24, 2012, http://opinionator.blogs.nytimes.com/2012/03/24
/the-brain-on-love/.

15. Ibid.

16. Ibid.

17. Ibid.

18. Quote was included in a book review by Laura Landro of *The Emotional Life of
Your Brain* by Richard J. Davidson and Sharon Begley, *The Wall Street Journal,*
March 5, 2012, http://online.wsj.com/article/SB10001424052970204571404577257713834265838.html.

Chapter Ten

1. Siegel, *Mindful Brain*, CD-ROM, Disc 1.

2. Ibid., Disc 4.

3. Ibid.

4. Ibid.

5. Walpola Rahula, *What the Buddha Taught* (New York: Grove/Atlantic, 1974), 69.

6. Siegel, *Mindful Brain*, CD-ROM, Disc 1.

7. Ibid.

8. Ibid., Disc 4.

9. Ibid., Discs 3, 4.

10. Ibid., Disc 4.

11. Siegel, *Reflections*, 13.

12. Ibid., 12.

13. Jonah Lehrer, "The Forgetting Pill: How a New Drug Can Target Your Worst Memories—and Erase Them Forever," *Wired*, March 2012, http://www.wired.com/magazine/2012/02/ff_forgettingpill/.

14. Ibid.

15. Ibid.

16. Ibid.

17. Definition from MedicineNet.com.

18. Curran, *About the Brain,* 157.

19. Ibid., 160.

20. Siegel, *Mindful Brain*, CD-ROM, Disc 4.

21. Ibid.

Chapter Fifteen

1. Jeffrey M. Lance, Ph.D., "Attachment and the Repetition Compulsion," therapyinla.com, December 2001, http://www.therapyinla.com/articles/article1201.html.

2. Ackerman, "Brain on Love."

Chapter Seventeen

1. Definition from TheFreeDictionary.com by Farlex.

2. Elisabeth Kübler-Ross and David Kessler, "The Five Stages of Grief," Grief.com, http://grief.com/the-five-stages-of-grief/.

3. Siegel, *Mindful Brain*, CD-ROM, Disc 3.

4. Ibid.

Chapter Eighteen

1. From a personal interview with Ram Dass in 1991.

2. Ibid.

3. Ibid.

4. Ibid.

5. UCLA Mindful Awareness Research Center, "Mindful Awareness Practices (MAPs for Daily Living)," Class Handouts: Week 3: Loving Kindness. For more information, see http://marc.ucla.edu/body.cfm?id=85.

6. Ibid.

7. Ibid.

Chapter Nineteen

1. Definition from TheFreeDictionary.com by Farlex, which also credits *Mosby's Medical Dictionary*, 8th edition (Elsevier, 2008).

Conclusion

1. From a personal interview with Ram Dass in 1991.

2. Ibid.

INDEX

..... 🧠 .....

ABOUT THE AUTHORS

..... 🧠 .....

Steven J. Fogel has been described as a "Renaissance man for the new millennium." He is a cofounder of Westwood Financial Corp., one of the leading private commercial real estate owners in the country. For decades he has been an active participant in the human potential movement, inspiring and mentoring others to seek their true selves. As a longtime student of human behavior and development, he has studied with psychologists, educators, and rabbinical scholars. Steve is an accomplished artist and the author of *The Yes-I-Can Guide to Mastering Real Estate*, published by Random House, and *My Mind Is Not My Friend: A Guide for How Not to Get in Your Own Way*, published by Fresh River Press. His broad experience in business and the arts led him to serve as chairman of the California Arts Council. He lives and works in Los Angeles.

Mark Bruce Rosin is the author of *Stepfathering* (Simon & Schuster and Ballantine) and coauthor, with Steven Jay Fogel, of

The Yes-I-Can Guide to Mastering Real Estate (Random House) and *My Mind Is Not Always My Friend* (Fresh River Press), and, with Glenn O. Turner, M.D., *Recognizing and Surviving Heart Attacks and Strokes: Lifesaving Advice You Need Now* (University of Missouri Press). Mark has served as a literary consultant and editor on many books, including Rod Stryker's *The Four Desires: Creating a Life of Purpose, Happiness, Prosperity, and Freedom* (Delacorte), a finalist for the 2011 Books for a Better Life Award in the motivation category, and Larry Moss's *The Intent to Live* (Bantam). Mark began his career in publishing as a contributing editor at *Harper's Bazaar* and a senior editor of *Parents* magazine, where he specialized in articles about psychology and child development. He is also an accomplished screenwriter.